101 THINGS

I WISH I KNEW

WHEN I GOT

MARRIED

101 THINGS
I WISH I KNEW
WHEN I GOT
MARRIED

SIMPLE LESSONS TO MAKE LOVE LAST

LINDA AND CHARLIE BLOOM

New World Library
Novato, California

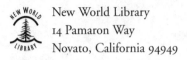

New World Library
14 Pamaron Way
Novato, California 94949

Edited by Kristen Cashman
Front cover design by Cathey Flickinger
Type design and typography by Tona Pearce Myers

Library of Congress Cataloging-in-Publication Data
Bloom, Linda,
  101 things I wish I knew when I got married : simple lessons to make love last / Linda and Charlie Bloom.
      p.   cm.
ISBN 1-57731-424-7 (pbk. : alk. paper)
1. Marriage. 2. Love. I. Title: One hundred one things I wish I knew when I got married. II. Title: One hundred and one things I wish I knew when I got married. III. Bloom, Charlie. IV. Title.
HQ734.B6573 2003
306.81—dc22   2003021608

First printing, February 2004
ISBN 1-57731-424-7
Printed in Canada on partially recycled, acid-free paper
Distributed to the trade by Publishers Group West

20 19 18 17 16 15 14 13 12

On March 1, 2001, while we were working on the first draft of this book, we got the phone call every parent prays they will never receive. Our son Eben had died in an accident. He was twenty-two. In the aftermath of the overwhelming grief that we both went through in the ensuing months, we found a source of life-giving strength in the love that we had been nurturing together over the years. The 102nd thing that we didn't know when we got married is that the love that two people share can get them through unspeakable suffering and help them both to heal from even the most terrible tragedies of their lives.

We dedicate this book to our beloved son Eben.

For one human being to love another; that is perhaps the most difficult of all our tasks; the ultimate, the last test and proof, the work for which all other work is but preparation.

— Rainer Maria Rilke

Contents

Acknowledgments

First and foremost we wish to thank our students and clients who have believed in us enough to put their faith and trust in us over the years. Thank you also for the courage you demonstrate in taking on the practices that committed partnerships require. You have been our teachers and our inspiration.

To our children, Jesse, Sarah, and Eben: thank you for your patience with us over the years, particularly during the early years when we were still struggling with our own unlearned lessons. You taught us forgiveness and self-forgiveness, over and over again.

To our friends and teachers, Stephen and Ondrea Levine, we have a special debt of gratitude. Thank you for reminding us that we are so much more than our emotions and desires, for teaching us to keep our hearts open in hell, and for helping us to awaken and strengthen the spirit that infuses our lives and our connection. Thanks also to Jack Kornfield for teaching us the practice of mindfulness, and to Thich Nhat Hanh for the "How can I best love you?" meditation, and for being a living embodiment of compassion. Thanks to Barry and Joyce Vissell, who helped to pull us back from the edge of the well on more than one occasion.

We also have a deep sense of gratitude to Nancy Lunney, who believed in us and our work and who invited us to teach at Esalen Institute, our second home. We cherish our dear friends who supported our dream of writing this book: Seymour Boorstein, David Kerns, John Amodeo, Claire Bloom, Susan Campbell, Connie Zweig, Lewis Engel, Kim Karkos, Lynn Gallo, Mary Melkonian, Sharon Savage, Monica Dashwood, and Grace Llewelyn. Without your belief in us, we couldn't have kept going with the project.

To Marc Allen and the wonderful staff at New World Library, especially our gifted editor, Kristen Cashman, and Georgia Hughes, Cathey Flickinger, Monique Muhlenkamp, and Munro Magruder: thank you for your enthusiastic support and expert guidance, and for creating a publishing house that is truly committed to service.

Foreword

Most of us, when we fall in love, simultaneously stumble into a multitude of myths, such as being "meant for each other" and "living happily ever after." Take a deep, forgiving breath and acknowledge any of the romantic movies you've conspired to create in your own life. Many of us awaken, as Dorothy did in *The Wizard of Oz,* in an unfamiliar land, discovering smoke and illusion behind passion's curtain, rather than what we most need to sustain real love. Relationships look pretty easy in the movies and on television, where most of us have learned what little we think we know about partnerships. The reality, we quickly learn, is different. The statistics about divorce are sobering, but they don't unearth the source of the problem.

We have surveyed many groups of seminar participants who confirm that most people have more training in driving a car than driving a successful relationship. No wonder people have such a hard time sustaining love! We have traveled the equivalent of thirty times around the world sharing stories and skills with couples. Everywhere we go, we hear the same question: How can I create a relationship that really works? Linda and Charlie Bloom have confronted that question squarely in their own partnership and in their seminars. What they share with you here is real — real knowledge about the real skills; that's what *101 Things I Wish I Knew When I Got Married* is all about.

"If only..." is a phrase we have all heard countless times. "If only I had known her better." "If only we had a chance to learn something about making love work." "If only we knew how to listen to each other." This illuminating book erases "If only." Here you'll find practical ways to connect and reconnect. You'll find the skills and the support to step into the unknown areas so that your relationship can flourish.

What's really delicious about Linda and Charlie's book is its bite-sized format. You can open the book to any page and find a nourishing morsel. As you digest theme after theme, you'll find that your relationship blossoms without the necessity to work hard or struggle. What a novel idea!

There is profound wisdom here that couples really need in order to succeed. The Blooms address the questions people ask most frequently in a way that will make you breathe easier and see your partner in a new light. Imagine having a relationship map with all the bumps and detours clearly illustrated. Imagine learning a new language for relationships gently, alongside a good friend. Linda and Charlie Bloom are insightful guides, and we're delighted to recommend their work to anyone seeking to take relationships to a new level.

Kathlyn and Gay Hendricks
Authors of *Conscious Loving* and *Lasting Love*

Introduction

CHARLIE: In February of 1999, my sister, Claire, called me from Los Angeles to inform me that she and her boyfriend, Mike, were going to get married. She asked me if I would be willing to pick out a passage related to marriage and read it at the ceremony. Of course, I accepted her request and immediately set out to come up with the right piece. I found lots of great quotes, poems, and stories, any of which probably would have worked fine. The problem was that none of them fully expressed what I wanted to say. They all spoke about aspects of a marriage — devotion, commitment, the benefits, the joys, the challenges — but each addressed only one facet of the whole.

What I wanted to give Claire and Mike was a more complete picture of all that marriage can be and what is required to realize that potential. Linda encouraged me to stop seeking other people's words and instead come up with my own. So I began listing some of the things I wished I had known when I got married. By sharing the lessons that Linda and I had learned through being together for thirty years, I hoped to spare Claire and Mike some of the suffering and struggling that we had experienced.

I came up with over fifty one-liners, but for time's sake, I cut it down to twenty-five. The ceremony was beautiful, and I got to share all of my insights, while the nods, winks, chuckles, and elbow pokes of the congregation punctuated my delivery. Afterward, several people, including the minister, asked me for copies of my notes. A few suggested that I expand them and think about getting them published. On the eight-hour drive home, Linda and I came up with more one-liners. By the end of the trip, we had eighty. Two weeks later, we had over a hundred. Eventually we came up with nearly two hundred. (I guess that says something about how much we *didn't* know when we got married.) We picked out what we considered to be the best of the bunch and ran them by a few of our friends who were either writers or therapists or both. The response was very favorable, but practically without exception our readers had one recommendation: include a couple of paragraphs of commentary with each one in order to flesh it out.

We decided to use a combination of anecdotes from our own marriage and those from clients, friends, and students, being certain of course to disguise the identities of everyone except ourselves. Having shared many of the details of our struggles with workshop participants for nearly twenty years, we have learned to use our experiences, mistakes, and discoveries as a means of helping couples to avoid — or at least extricate themselves from — some of the pitfalls, breakdowns, impasses, quagmires, and other difficulties that inevitably arise during the course of a marriage.

Though Linda and I are both trained marriage counselors, each with over twenty-five years of experience, the vast majority of what we present in this book comes from our personal experience, not from what we learned in graduate school. Our qualifications are not hanging in framed certificates on our walls, but rather are the scars and wounds that we have experienced, endured, and subsequently learned and recovered from.

"That which doesn't kill me," Friedrich Nietzsche said, "makes me stronger." So it seems to be with marriage: we either learn to grow through the inevitable challenges of a committed partnership, or we risk being broken by them. Linda and I have probably experienced as much stress and struggle as most of our many friends who have divorced. Our clients and students have presented very few problems to us that we haven't endured ourselves. We have come close to losing our marriage on several occasions, and each time we managed to pull back from the edge, rather than going over it. It's been several years now since our marriage has experienced one of those near-death experiences, and at this point it seems unlikely that it will again. There are, however, no guarantees even for the best marriages, and the surest way to jeopardize a great relationship is to take it for granted and put it on cruise control.

LINDA: Both of us feel blessed to share the partnership we have today, but it hasn't come easily; our mature love was hard-won. When Charlie spoke at Claire and Mike's wedding, I felt proud of what we had accomplished together. We had survived enough crises and endured enough ordeals to be able to speak with some authority about the possibilities and pitfalls of marriage. Charlie was offering his sister and her new husband what we both wished had been offered to us. It would have saved us a lot of suffering if we had learned and embodied these truths earlier. There were so many times in our relationship when we had floundered, when I wished I'd had a wise relative to whom I could turn for advice and who could help us out of the confusion. Not having such a family member to consult, I turned to spiritual teachers, workshops, tapes, authors, therapists, and friends and tried to figure it out on my own. I hope to provide guidance for people seeking it, as I was.

During our first few years together, Charlie and I knew what kind of relationship we desired, but it took more than vision to bring it to fruition. We were up against conditioned patterns and lifelong habits. Neutralizing them would take practice, devotion, and time. Determined that we could do it, I held fast to my vision and commitment.

Many factors contributed to the difficulties we experienced, particularly during the early years of our marriage. We were both only twenty-one when we began our relationship, and quite immature. Each of us was looking for someone to provide us with emotional security, since neither of us had developed any real sense of wholeness within ourselves. We had very distorted pictures of what love is. We weren't equipped to participate in a healthy relationship; neither of us had seen examples of them in our families or been very successful in any of our previous relationships. We were each looking for someone to help us get free from the pain of our pasts. Our first child was born less than two years after we got married, when we were both full-time graduate students, saddled with debt and both out of work. The stress level was almost unbearable at times.

And then there were all the vast differences between us. Although most couples tend to complement each other with their differences, ours have always seemed inordinately extreme. In most personality traits, we represent opposite ends of the spectrum: I am detailed-oriented, Charlie is a generalist; I favor strict parenting, Charlie doesn't; I am an outgoing, social person, Charlie is more of an introvert; I go to bed early, he stays up late; I like to get to the airport with hours to spare, a fifteen-minute wait is too much for him; I believe in planning and preparation, Charlie favors spontaneity; I seek connection when I am stressed, Charlie solitude; my strength is commitment, Charlie's is letting go; when we teach, I use notes, while he prefers to wing it; I'm a talker, he's a thinker; I manage money, he spends it. The list goes on, but you get the idea. Over the years, people have asked us countless times, "How did you guys ever get together? And how did you *stay* together?"

In the early years of our marriage, because neither of us knew how to deal with our differences, we frequently found ourselves in conflict. It wasn't the differences themselves that kept getting us in trouble, but our reactions to them. Like many couples, we attempted to do away with our differences by trying to change each other or ourselves. Homogenizing our personalities, and thus eliminating the sources of conflict, seemed at the time to be a good idea. This strategy, we were to eventually discover, doesn't work. Instead, it produced further conflict, both within ourselves and between us.

There was, of course, more to our relationship than suffering and struggle. Had there not been, we could not and would not have stayed together. From our earliest days, a deeply loving connection has sustained us through the ordeals, the power struggles, the disappointments, and even the betrayals. We shared experiences as a couple and as a family that were joyous beyond measure.

Even the strongest bonds, however, are not immune to the toll that ongoing struggles can impose on the relationship. For us, the turning point came in 1987, after fifteen years of marriage. Conflict and frustration had worn us down to the point where we both were questioning whether it was worth it to go on together. As much as each of us wanted to preserve our marriage and our family, the strain of dealing with irreconcilable differences was getting to be too much. We reached a point where we could see why couples who love each other choose divorce. For both of us there was sadness and relief in that recognition; we were grief-stricken that we seemed to be about to lose our marriage but simultaneously relieved that the struggle might be coming to an end. Fortunately, facing the reality of divorce led us to realize what we stood to lose and how much we both really wanted to preserve it. We knew there had to be another way, and that helped us make the leap from tolerating our differences to appreciating them.

Attempting to dissolve our differences hadn't worked, so we began trying instead to meet them with acceptance, gratitude, and appreciation and to see if we could find the hidden gifts in them. We knew, at least intellectually, that it was these differences that had drawn us and made us attractive to each other. At the same time, they were the primary source of what triggered our reactive patterns. Thus we discovered that what drove us crazy about each other and what we were crazy about in each other were one and the same thing. The challenge was neither to try to change the other nor be willing to change for them, but rather to honor our own uniqueness while strengthening the bonds of loving respect between us. Learning to see our differences as tools for becoming more loving and fulfilled, rather than as obstacles to be overcome, denied, or eliminated, has profoundly altered how we relate to each other and everyone else in our lives. In our work with couples, we have found that while it does require effort and intention to adopt this orientation, it need not take as long as it took us to do so.

The experiences that brought us to our knees made us the people we are, and the learning and recovery that went along with each one have shaped our relationship into the treasure it is now. Through the many unskillful ways we treated each other, we learned the meaning of true respect. Because we were hanging by threads so many times, at risk of separation and divorce, we learned to truly care for each other, the relationship, and ourselves. From having come so close to the edge, we have learned to love with an enormous sense of gratitude. Although the lessons we have learned in this process have not come easily, the rewards of our efforts are sweet: an abundance of harmony, ease, and joy. We hope that this book will not only help you to appreciate the power of this perspective, but also assist you in applying it to your own relationships.

101 Things I Wish I Knew When I Got Married is for anyone who is, has been, or will be in a committed partnership. It is for anyone who has ever sensed that marriage can be much more than an arrangement of convenience for the purpose of managing obligations, responsibilities, and personal needs. It is for anyone who is unwilling to settle for less than the full measure of riches available in a life of true partnership, and who trusts that the prices of this undertaking, formidable though they may appear to be, are insignificant in comparison with the indescribable benefits to oneself, one's family, and the world that stand to be gained.

We are two ordinary people who, through a combination of good luck, good help, hard work, commitment, and a steadfast faith in a shared vision, made it through the ordeals of marriage and learned from our experiences. We are no different from anyone else, and if we can do it, so can you. We don't tell you what to do in these pages, but we offer you our confidence in the power of your own intention and our trust in the human capacity to heal from a wounded past and, in so doing, to become even stronger. As we have both discovered, it is the wounds themselves that enable us to develop the qualities that bring joy and love more fully into our lives.

We have both been inspired by our clients, students, and teachers to create this series of guidelines that distill down to essence the principles that have allowed our relationship to flourish. For young couples just starting out in their marriages, may these lessons save them some trouble. For long-established couples, may our advice provide a new perspective on the ingredients of a successful marriage.

From our experience, the deepest satisfaction that life has to offer comes from our most intimate relationships. By taking on the challenges of a committed partnership we are prompted to realize the fullness of our being. More than any other relationship, marriage has the potential to awaken our deepest longings and needs, as well as our deepest pains and fears. In learning to meet all of these powerful forces with an open heart and with authenticity, we can grow ourselves into wholeness, maturity, and compassion. In one of his workshops, Stephen Levine, the author of *Embracing the Beloved,* called marriage the "ultimate danger sport." People can, he said, learn more about themselves in a week in a relationship than by sitting in meditation in a cave for a year. Having tried both marriage and meditation, we'd have to agree. The development of self-awareness and self-knowledge is both the means to and the end of a good marriage. The process is simple but not easy. Our hope is that this book will more fully open your heart and mind to the inexpressible treasures available on the path of relationship.

101 THINGS
I WISH I KNEW
WHEN I GOT
MARRIED

1

*Great relationships
don't just happen;
they are created.*

The exemplary marriages we know of have been earned. These relationships are true partnerships, built on foundations of hard-won trust that accrues over time. The struggles and efforts to reconcile what can often appear to be impossible differences create the groundwork for these marriages. While compatibility and shared interests bring us together initially, they are not enough to keep us together over time. If there are no breakdowns, there is not enough friction and agitation to prompt development. We don't need to seek stress; life brings it right to us. Invariably, obstacles arise that lovers have to overcome. Challenges vary from a family's disapproval of the union to health problems or financial difficulties to differing styles, values, and belief systems. As the committed couple meets these challenges with their com-bined resources, the relationship becomes stronger and more resilient.

Meaningful events link together and accumulate over the years: a gentle touch to comfort us when we are agitated, an intimate conversation, shared laughter, a cup of tea when we are exhausted, a bowl of soup when we are sick, special care to make the sexual experience extra thrilling, a show of pride in our partner's achievements, acts of forgiveness, and all the precious moments of connection, insight, compassion, and understanding. These interactions are the building blocks of a great love erected over time.

One of the most important things we can do to keep our relationship strong and healthy is build the bond of affec-tion. It starts as a thin cord and grows ever thicker and stronger. When the inevitable stresses of life befall us in the form of differences and disappointments, the cord can become frayed. Gradually, with conscious choice, commit-ment, and intention, we can repair the connective cord with sincere acts of consideration, generosity, and kindness on a daily basis.

Creating a storehouse of goodwill in the relationship is like putting money in the bank. These deposits can take many forms — a conversation, an episode of working out differences, a lingering gaze, or a sincere expression of grati-tude — but they all have the common end of reaffirming our love and commitment, and they accumulate into a big tally. When there is an abundant account, you can make with-drawals when times are hard, and you live life with peace of mind, relishing a growing emotional wealth.

2

*Vulnerability
is disarming.*

LINDA: Arguments don't end when one person overpowers another. Bringing out the big guns — threats, name-calling, insults, loud yelling — always exacts a painfully high price. We may intimidate our partner into submission, thus winning the battle for momentary dominance, but this does not win us the war. It's a temporary truce, which creates tension because the conflict has merely been driven underground. The cost is a loss of trust, goodwill, caring, and respect.

For years, I reacted to Charlie's unsolicited criticism of me with counter-criticism. This reactive pattern never resulted in either of us feeling accepted or understood. So what if we were both right? It didn't matter. It wasn't until I stopped saying, "You never listen to me," and, "You always have to be right," that the impasse between us began to dissolve. Instead,

I said, "I really want us to understand each other, and it's so painful for me when we don't connect." When I revealed my own frustration and pain rather than "correcting" Charlie's responses, the tension between us softened and we were better able to hear each other.

To move toward resolution during times of distress, we need to do what we desire most to avoid — find the courage to be vulnerable. The peace of understanding will not result from efforts to get our partner to back down, stop fighting, and listen to us. It will instead result from the openness that arises when we are willing to disarm ourselves of our verbal defenses. Personal disarmament is the act of standing undefended and speaking the heart's truth even in the face of fear.

The more I practiced, the less fearful I felt, and the more natural it became for me to drop my guard. I found that courageous honesty almost always brings forth the same from the other person. But regardless of how our partner responds to us, undefended communication is itself a transformative gift to ourselves as well as to our relationship. In honoring our truth, we deepen the development of self-trust, self-worth, and self-respect, while simultaneously bringing greater honesty and integrity into our marriage. When we give what we desire to receive, the process always becomes its own reward.

Vulnerability provides us with greater integrity and greater access to our own heart and the deeper truth of our own experience. Speaking from vulnerability connects us with ourselves and creates a safe climate for our mutual love and tenderness to blossom. That's a success in itself. The gift to our partner is our openheartedness — the access to our sweet, kind, warm feelings that lie just beneath the surface of the criticisms and conflict.

3

If your job gets your best energy, your marriage will wither.

Phillip's parents divorced when he was four. His mother and two sisters raised him. His mother never remarried, and the family struggled financially throughout Phillip's childhood. While growing up he continually vowed that he would never be poor again and that his children would never lack any material thing they wanted. He married Eileen, who recognized in Phillip a man of not only great ambition, but also kindness and compassion. However, she also saw that his childhood experience had left him with unhealed emotional wounds. She loved him deeply and felt certain that her love would mend the insecurity that drove him to strive so relentlessly to succeed.

When her efforts failed to neutralize Phillip's hyper-ambition, Eileen became resentful and frustrated, often accusing him of caring more about his business than their family.

"That's not true," he would insist, "I'm committed to the family, and I don't want the kids to go through what I went through growing up. You don't appreciate what I'm doing for you. You're ungrateful."

Phillip's defensiveness and Eileen's frustration created a stalemate that seemed unbreakable. But the real problem was that they had polarized one another, taking opposing positions that made it seem as though Phillip had to choose between favoring work over family, or vice versa. It was as though both Eileen and Phillip were hypnotized into seeing things as either/or. This view made it impossible for either of them to hear each other's true perspectives.

The impasse broke one day when Eileen decided to stop criticizing Phillip. She refrained from calling him an uncaring workaholic and instead began speaking from the pain of her own broken heart. She told him how much she missed him and how sad she was that the children were growing up without the presence of a loving dad, just as he had. She didn't want him to give up his work, only to open up more time to include the family. She replaced the sting of her anger with the softness of her love. As a result, Phillip gradually became more able to hear her without becoming defensive or angry. For the first time, he was able to see the possibility that he could have both his work and his family. From that point on, Eileen and Phillip worked as partners in cocreating a life that worked for all of the family. Although there were occasional setbacks and difficulties, they never again reverted to the antagonistic pattern that nearly destroyed their marriage.

*One of the greatest gifts
you can give your partner
is your own happiness.*

CHARLIE: Like many of us, I grew up with the notion that marriage requires self-sacrifice. I believed that successful couples put each other's needs ahead of their own and forego pleasures that their mate doesn't share. It's no wonder I wasn't exactly jumping out of my skin to settle down. In the shadow of my independent, commitment-averse self was the side of me that craved connection, affection, and (let's be honest) regular sex. So, at the age of twenty-five I got married. Given my beliefs, it's not surprising that my feelings were somewhat mixed when Linda and I tied the knot. In one candid wedding photo, my look of consternation exposes this ambivalence.

For me, the hard part of marriage was deconstructing the beliefs that I had been caught up in and creating a life in which I could experience real happiness. With time, effort, and support, this intention has been, for the most part, fulfilled, largely due to the help I've received from Linda. She gave me the encouragement and trust that I was often unable to give myself along the way. Linda helped me to see that I didn't have to become a martyr and sacrifice myself in order to make our marriage work. She showed me that my responsibility to create a fulfilling, joyful life for myself was as important as anything that I could do for her or the kids. "The greatest gift you can give us is your own happiness," she said. "We don't want a husband and a dad who feels unhappy and burdened, no matter what else you're bringing home." I had to hear that message many times and in many ways before I finally understood it.

I learned that my inner responsibilities to myself were as important as my outer responsibilities to others. I came to trust that the quality of my own life is no less important than the quality of my family members'. It is my job, not Linda's or anyone else's, to see to it that my needs are met and that I experience fulfillment in my life. This has probably been the most valuable lesson I've ever learned, and it's one that I keep relearning at deeper levels. I've come to see that responsibility, in the truest sense of the word — responsibility for oneself — isn't an obligation or burden, but a gift and a blessing.

Most of us come into a marriage looking for what we can get from the arrangement. Love, attention, security, pleasure, companionship, and distraction from unpleasant feelings or thoughts are some of the things that compel us into partnership. When we no longer hold our partner responsible for the fulfillment of our needs, everything changes. This is easier said than done, but it is perhaps the single most important thing we can do to ensure that our relationship will be mutually satisfying. Taking care of ourselves isn't selfish; it's the most generous and responsible thing we can do.

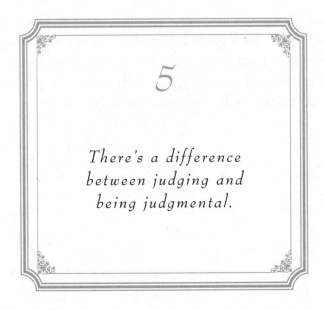

5

*There's a difference
between judging and
being judgmental.*

Conscious living requires us to make assessments. We assess risk level, cost benefits, and appropriateness of behaviors in specific situations. We have to make certain judgment calls every day. We make judgments in our relationships too, but we sometimes forget that they are personal, temporary evaluations, instead viewing them as objectively, permanently true. Being judgmental in a relationship is usually disastrous because once we attach ourselves to a fixed characterization of our partner, we have a very hard time letting go of that assessment and seeing them differently.

Paul made up his mind to improve his relationship. He ordered self-help tapes and books and immersed himself in them. He took on the challenge of waking up each day with a total commitment to his marriage. What he was learning began to show up in his relationship with Cookie. He brought her flowers, he stopped watching TV after work to ask about her day, he stopped expecting her to wait on him, he was attentive to their grandchild when she came to visit. But no matter what he did, Cookie continued to view him from her old perspective. It was as if she had taken a snapshot of Paul years ago and glued it into the photo album of her mind. She couldn't turn the page but still had it open to the same old picture and kept staring at it. Cookie was lying in wait for evidence that Paul couldn't be trusted. Since no one is perfect, of course, she found it. One day, when Paul slipped and told her to bring his coffee, Cookie confronted him with the accusation that he really hadn't changed.

After a while Paul began to feel like there wasn't any point in trying because he knew that sooner or later he was bound to lapse into an old behavior and Cookie would condemn him once again. Although he initially began to change his behavior for the sake of the marriage, he was now doing it for himself. He realized he had no control over how Cookie viewed him. Her intractable view of Paul made her the bigger loser. Being attached to her judgments prevented her from appreciating the changes Paul was making. She couldn't see that their relationship had actually improved. Her attachment to her judgments was so strong that it prevented her from seeing the part she was playing in their relationship being stuck.

When Paul eventually told Cookie that he was no longer willing to keep trying to prove his love, Cookie took this as another piece of evidence that he didn't really care and had been pretending all along. Shortly thereafter, Paul made the judgment call that he was unable to persuade Cookie to recognize his love for her as sincere. Cookie's judgments of Paul kept her expectations of him to a minimum, thus protecting her from the pain of disappointment. This couple did stay married, but they were never really happy together. Ultimately, Cookie's attachment to her judgments prevented them both from experiencing a satisfying and fulfilling connection.

6

*It's possible
to hate and love someone
at the same time.*

LINDA: Loving someone doesn't mean that we always have warm and wonderful feelings toward them. Love is a stew flavored by a variety of ingredients — sometimes sweetness, spice, bitterness, or saltiness, and sometimes "the works." Our ever-changing feelings, whether they are pleasurable or painful, do not reflect the underlying nature of our relationship. In a marriage, strong emotions are inevitable. If we can accept them without judgment of our partner or ourselves, they can float freely and open us to yet unawakened parts of ourselves. The presence of so-called negative feelings is not the problem. It is how we respond to them within ourselves and in reaction to each other that determines whether they will deepen or diminish our love. Accepting all of the feelings that arise in a committed partnership allows us to learn to love more fully and deeply.

I remember a time in our relationship when Charlie broke an agreement that was very important to me. At the time, our children were small and we had agreed to share in their care. Charlie's new job required that he be out of town more than he was home. I had supported him in accepting the job, but his absences had become longer and more frequent than either of us had expected. I found myself in the position of being our children's sole caregiver. I was furious! How could he be so selfish and inconsiderate? What kind of a jerk had I gotten involved with, anyway? Did I really want to stay with him? This was more than simple anger; it was hatred. At least that's how I felt at the time. And yet even in the midst of my "in-burst" (in those days I kept most of my angry feelings to myself), I remember distinctly hearing another voice within me saying, "and you love this guy." I can remember the confusion I felt when I realized that right along with the burning hatred was the very same love I was familiar with. My customary simplistic thinking — good/bad, right/wrong, black/white, either/or — was challenged. Somehow it seemed wrong for hate and love to occur simultaneously, but there they both were. I was challenged to learn how to hold the tension of the opposites.

Although my mind couldn't make sense of this paradox, my heart knew that it was reality. While in this moment of extreme anger, even rage, toward Charlie, I knew that the intensity of my emotions was due to the depth of my love and passion for him. Although I still get angry at Charlie sometimes, it usually moves through me very quickly, and then once again I'm assured of the vast love that underlies all of my feelings.

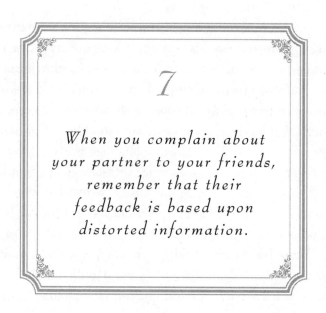

7

*When you complain about
your partner to your friends,
remember that their
feedback is based upon
distorted information.*

Everyone in Joan's life was telling her to get a divorce. Her husband, Greg, had been having an affair for months. His dishonesty was more painful to Joan than the affair itself. She doubted that she would ever be able to trust him again. "Get rid of him!" her sister pleaded. "Once a cheater, always a cheater," her best friend told her. Joan's loved ones meant well, but they were biased. They were distressed to see her in so much pain, and they wanted the old Joan back again. Normally strong, Joan was now having trouble keeping her life together. To observers, it can appear that there are clear-cut perpetrators and victims. On closer investigation, however, there is usually more to the story.

Joan had played a part in the demise of the marriage. She had not been receiving the emotional support she desired and had been angry and cold toward Greg for a long time. Freezing him out was her way of making him pay. She had allowed their facade of a marriage to go on. Neither Joan nor Greg addressed their difficulties in a straightforward fashion. These two had silently, unconsciously conspired to create a context that let their marriage deteriorate. This fact certainly does not justify Greg's infidelity, but Joan was complicit in creating conditions in the marriage that gave rise to his affair. Until she was able to recognize this, as well as her intention to punish him by withholding her deeper feelings, the healing process could never begin.

Joan's friends and family were reacting from a limited point of view of right and wrong, good and bad, black and white. It's a lot to ask of our friends and family to see a more complex picture, but if we want support of the highest caliber, that's what we need to do. We can instead say, "Please don't take sides. The best way you can assist me is to help me see my part in this breakdown." Otherwise, we may be better off not telling them our one-sided version of the story.

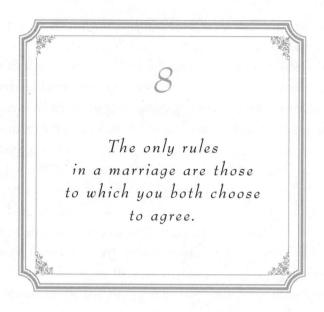

8

*The only rules
in a marriage are those
to which you both choose
to agree.*

Any policies and practices that both partners are in accord with may be workable in a marriage, as long as they don't cause harm to anyone. We may wish to modify agreements as conditions and perspectives change over time. If we bring a discerning eye to our experience, we can reassess the consequences of our agreements and fine-tune, reshape, or eliminate altogether whatever we decide isn't working.

Ellen was an accomplished attorney who earned more money than her husband, Herb. After Ellen gave birth to twin girls, she and Herb decided that Herb would be the one to leave his job to stay home with the children. Both sets of in-laws had judgments about the nontraditional choice they were making. Some of their friends commented that it struck them as peculiar that Herb was "Mr. Mom." They were worried that he wouldn't fit the role he was taking on. Despite some misgivings, Herb and Ellen implemented their plan. Herb stayed home with the kids and Ellen provided the family's sole source of income. The girls blossomed in Herb's capable care. He loved being home with them, and Ellen was able to maintain a good connection with the family without having to give up the career that gave her so much gratification. Herb remained the primary caregiver until the girls started kindergarten, and then he went back to work. Despite the judgments of relatives and friends, the family thrived.

We all grow up with certain fixed ideas about marriage. It's easy to forget that many of these notions do not represent how things *have* to be but are instead subject to interpretation and modification. While religious and social traditions are helpful in establishing a marriage's operating principles, the relationship runs the risk of losing vitality and passion when it fails to incorporate the ever-changing needs and concerns of each partner. Marriage is not a fixed entity but a work in progress, inviting ongoing refinement. Good marriages are not likely to thrive when built upon unexamined traditions. They flourish when they are continually cocreated by both partners.

9

Commitment isn't a prison;
it's a means to
greater freedom.

CHARLIE: When I shared this observation with my single friend Howard, he looked at me as though I had taken permanent leave of my senses. I don't blame him for his reaction. Not long before that, I had the same association with the dreaded "C word." It wasn't until after Linda and I had been together for several years that I stopped feeling like I was stuck in a trap and began to experience the liberating nature of true commitment.

Before that, the problem was that I was not really committed in the marriage. Sure, I tried to keep the promises and vows that we agreed would define our relationship, but that was more a matter of honoring the word than understanding the spirit of our agreements. Most of the time, it felt more like going through the motions than really embracing the essence of the covenant. I hadn't surrendered my resistance, which manifested itself in second-guessing my decision to marry, envying other men who weren't tied down, and feeling resentful for having missed out on more time to sow my wild oats. These thoughts often left me feeling sorry for myself. In those days I often found myself criticizing Linda and picking arguments to blow off my self-created dissatisfaction.

Thanks to a combination of perseverance, good help, supportive friends, understanding from Linda, and the maturity that comes from staying with something long enough, I eventually grew beyond my feelings of being trapped. I began to appreciate the many blessings and benefits of sharing a relationship with a loving, supportive partner. I came to value the security that comes from sharing a life with someone who knows you at your best and worst and who will not withdraw her support when you're having a bad day. I came to trust that I could not do anything to jeopardize Linda's love. This freed up vast amounts of energy that had formerly been locked into patterns of approval seeking that showed up not only in my primary relationship, but with others as well.

As our capacity to love each other grows, we become increasingly able to rest in the knowledge that we are loved for who we are, not what we do. Over time, we come to develop a previously unknown well of self-love. Feeling loved and really letting that in provides a fantastic freedom: freedom from fear of loss and freedom to be ourselves fully.

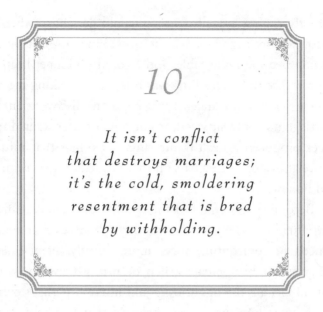

10

*It isn't conflict
that destroys marriages;
it's the cold, smoldering
resentment that is bred
by withholding.*

LINDA: As a little girl, I witnessed and experienced the pain caused by anger, and I adopted a strategy of compliance to protect myself from strong emotions. I knew that whenever feelings got too heated, someone was likely to get hurt, and it might be me. So I tried to ignore differences and avoid conflict whenever possible. When I did get angry, I buried the ugly emotion and pretended that everything was fine. I relied on this tactic well into my marriage, before I came to recognize its hidden costs. Although Charlie and I didn't argue a lot, I spent years feeling like a victim whenever we did, pitying myself and sizzling with resentment over how unfair our relationship seemed to be.

It was I, not Charlie, who wouldn't accept the angry feelings. When we did fight, it was often over my failure to honestly express myself. Charlie would get angry when he uncovered feelings I had been concealing. Eventually the tension became unbearable, and I could no longer keep up the pretense that everything was fine. Finally taking the risk of experiencing my anger, I was happy to discover that our marriage not only survived, it got much better. Our differences produced a healthy measure of conflict that infused our relationship with a passion that yielded deeper intimacy and honesty.

Becoming less afraid of the conflict that can arise from our differences is one of the wonderful bonuses that I experienced in confronting anger more directly. Now I don't cringe when I anticipate a flap occurring between us but instead feel a sense of curiosity and interest, perhaps even a touch of excitement. I never believed that I could lose my fear of conflict, but I have. To call this a miracle may seem a bit dramatic, but that's what it feels like to me!

11

*If you choose monogamy,
keep your agreement.*

CHARLIE: Perhaps no aspect of marriage is more provocative, challenging, and misunderstood than monogamy. More than an agreement for sexual exclusivity, monogamy is actually a shared commitment to consecrate marriage by containing our most intimate experiences within the relationship. The primary effect of this commitment is not a limiting of experience but a deepening of it.

When we invest sexual exclusivity in our relationship it gives us a chance to know and discover each other and ourselves in increasingly subtle and delightful ways. It brings a quality of ever-changing mystery into our lives. In a mutual, shared process like this, boredom and indifference cannot survive. A couple can experience excitement, passion, and surprise together even after sixty years.

When sexual energies are not focused in this way, even the intensity of a new romance can quickly fade to disinterest and flatness. When we feel a persistent desire to become sexual with someone else, the real question is not "What's wrong with my marriage, or my partner?" but "What kind of attention have we stopped bringing to each other?" and "What is the emptiness within me that I am hoping to fill with the excitement of a new infatuation?" When we transfer the energy and attention that a new romance unleashes to a commitment to a deeper level of truthfulness and intimacy in our marriage, the desire to be with another loses its grip on us.

Marital commitment is not easy to keep. Regardless of how much love we share with our partner, the desire for physical intimacy with others may continue to arise. If we don't view our resistance to temptation — our sacrifice — as the sacred offering that it is, we're likely to experience feelings of deprivation that can create resentment and self-pity, which might actually lead to sexual infidelity.

In the early years of our marriage I struggled, at times unsuccessfully, with my commitment to monogamy. So I know how tough it can be to maintain. Fortunately, Linda and I were able to heal the broken trust that resulted from my actions and repair the damage before things deteriorated too much. I doubt that we could have done this had I chosen to lie rather than acknowledge the truth to Linda. Working through these experiences helped us both rediscover our commitment to monogamy as a gift to each other rather than a hardship we were forced to endure. Desire and attraction to others still arise for me occasionally, but I have learned to manage them and avoid acting on my impulses.

In time, the commitment to monogamy becomes the practice through which we develop and strengthen many of the qualities that strong marriages require. When we take it on, we are agreeing to much more than sexual exclusivity. We are affirming that we will do whatever is within our power to maintain the highest possible degree of authenticity and integrity in our relationship. The rewards of a continuously evolving, ever-growing partnership become more compelling than temporary pleasure, which is tempting but much less satisfying.

Ultimately the question of monogamy is not a moral one. It's essentially a matter of enlightened self-interest. Keeping the agreement to monogamy provides a container within which we are able to experience greater depth and fulfillment in our marriage and greater levels of self-awareness and self-development.

12

*It's not what you've got;
it's what you do with it.*

Sugie was fifty-three years old when his mother died. He had never been married and had always lived with her. Her death was a grievous loss. Before she died, he had dated intermittently, but after her death, he committed himself to finding a wife. Sugie was not exactly the picture of an eligible bachelor. He was short, chubby, and bald, but he knew he had a great deal of love to give. He was tenacious in his attempts to locate a partner. When he had exhausted the possibilities in his small town in West Virginia, he went to Kentucky and began putting ads in the local paper in the town where some of his friends lived.

Tess was forty-eight when she answered Sugie's personal ad. She had lived all her life in the mountains. Both of her previous husbands had been coal miners who became ill early in life and died in their forties. What Sugie and Tess had in common was their grief and loneliness and their dream of someday finding a sweet love. When they met, they had an instant, powerful connection.

When Sugie and Tess take their daily walks at sunset, they go hand-in-hand. They are unspeakably pleased to have found each other. People who knew Sugie thought he would remain a bachelor for the rest of his life. They thought he was just "spinning yarns" when he spoke of "when I get married..." But Sugie knew in his quiet, determined way that someday he would manifest his heart's deepest desire. I remember what Sugie used to say: "I always knew that what Grandma Bertie told me was true. She always said, 'There's a lid for every pot.'"

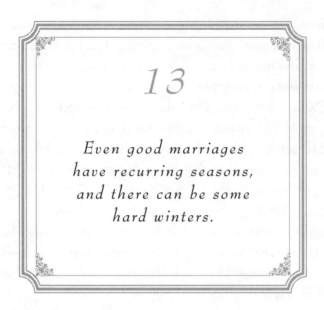

13

*Even good marriages
have recurring seasons,
and there can be some
hard winters.*

Under the influence of the "happily ever after" myth, we may have the illusion that good marriages are all sweetness and joy, without periods of darkness or pain. Being crazy about each other unfortunately doesn't guarantee long-term bliss or a conflict-free relationship. It can be a shock to discover that the level of trust can go up and down, as can the feelings of goodwill between partners. In every marriage, there will be some very difficult times. We may be averse to going through times of uncertainty, fear, disappointment, or even betrayal, and when the inevitable occurs, we may feel furious or stunned or doubtful about our marriage surviving this desolate period.

Our faith will be tested. This phenomenon occurs in all relationships, not just the "difficult" ones. Relationships that grow from, rather than succumb to, these ordeals are distinguished not by the depth of the challenges, but by the willingness of both partners to face them honestly and directly. This willingness promotes the strength that warms us during the cold season. Just as spring follows winter, we can move through the difficult period, and the relationship will be born anew.

Brandon and Suzanne were married with two children. They loved each other, but there was a serious problem: Brandon was addicted to gambling. Over time, Suzanne became overwhelmed with feelings of helplessness. Gradually her love became contaminated by resentment. She tried everything she could think of to influence Brandon, but nothing worked. His lies were as damaging to their marriage as his financial losses. Finally, Suzanne could barely stand to look at him anymore; they both knew that the marriage was over. They separated, initiating plans for a divorce. Brandon moved to a different community, and Suzanne stayed in their old house with the kids.

Without Suzanne's constant monitoring, Brandon plunged even deeper into his addiction. Although he expected to feel relieved and free without Suzanne's restraints, he instead experienced an overwhelming sense of loneliness and shame. Even gambling had lost the power to soothe his pain. He sank into his own private hell, finally hitting bottom. Out of his despair, he gradually found the motivation to change his life.

Brandon took the step, getting into therapy and joining Gamblers Anonymous. He eventually realized how his long-standing wounds had resulted in his need for constant stimulation and excitement. During his appointed times for visitation with the children, Brandon would attempt to make emotional contact with Suzanne. She remained cold and businesslike. He tried to tell her of his realizations and recovery, but she was closed to his efforts. He wrote her letters, but received none in return. Nevertheless, he kept trying. Brandon was on a serious campaign to win her back. He was convinced that he had substantively and permanently changed and was now worthy of her love and trust. He was determined to not just tell Suzanne this, but to show her. It was a long, harsh winter.

Spring eventually did arrive. A year and a half after the divorce, Suzanne's feelings toward Brandon began to thaw. She let herself begin to trust his words and actions, despite her fear of more betrayal and disappointment. Over time, she began to trust Brandon enough to let him move back in with the family, and two years after the divorce, they re-married. They had two more children, and Brandon has remained on the wagon for over ten years with no signs of falling off. More important, he has demonstrated his commitment to being a loving and responsible husband and father through his actions, not simply through his words. They currently share a marriage that is far more solid than the one they had before.

Most couples don't go through such a dramatic severance and reunification as Brandon and Suzanne, but nearly all endure some version of the death and rebirth cycle. Sometimes the coldest winter can precipitate the most joyful springtime renewal.

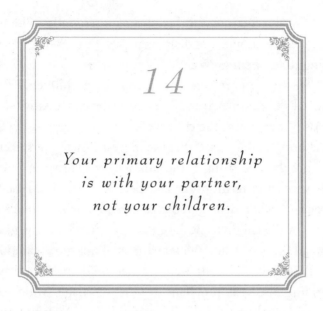

14

*Your primary relationship
is with your partner,
not your children.*

We don't serve the needs of our children when we neglect
our relationship to attend to them. It can sometimes feel as
if there is a competition for attention between our partner
and our kids. When we realize that the well-being of the children is directly related to the well-being of our marriage, we
are less apt to feel guilty or neglectful when we tend to our
primary relationship.

For Betty, the children always came first. She claimed
that since her husband Stefan was an adult, he could take
care of himself and shouldn't need much attention. Even as
her children grew into adolescence and young adulthood,
she never modified her position. She justified her stance by
saying to Stefan, "You're not giving enough to them, so I
need to."

"I'm not focusing on them," Stefan responded, "because they need to stand on their own two feet. When are you going to let them grow up?"

"You just don't care about your own children," Betty blurted through her tears. They had this conversation hundreds of times over the course of their marriage. Sadly, they were both unable to see that the biggest casualty of the crisis was not the well-being of the children, but of their marriage. For years, the relationship had been starving from lack of attention, while Betty and Stefan argued over their perceived needs of the children. Both of their children had now grown into adulthood, while the marriage had not grown at all.

Betty's relentless attention to her children was a way of avoiding the real problems in the marriage, which had become nearly devoid of affection and care. Stefan's unwillingness to feed the marriage by acknowledging his own loneliness and sadness served to perpetuate the pattern. Ironically but predictably, the children for whom Betty sacrificed her marriage were also losers in this game. Not only did they lose out on the kind of support they needed to become more independent and responsible people, but they missed the opportunity to grow up in the care of a loving partnership. As a result, neither of them was very hopeful about the prospects for their own successful marriage. Betty and Stefan managed to stay together even after their kids moved away from home, but their marriage remained unsatisfying because they never faced their real issues. They stayed together because it was easier to follow the old pattern and they were fearful of being alone.

One of the greatest gifts we can give our children is demonstrating a happy marriage. More than anything else we can do for them, this example supports and encourages the possibility of creating such a relationship in their own lives. The time to learn about the blessings of a marriage is not after the kids have left home. If we haven't done it by then, it's probably too late. The time to model a healthy marriage is throughout our children's development.

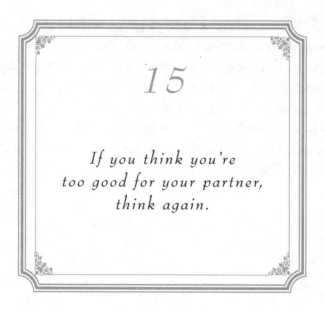

15

*If you think you're
too good for your partner,
think again.*

Fran and Erik married when they were both very young. Fran had been a "Daddy's girl," always doted on and indulged by a father who treated her as if she could do no wrong. Erik adored her and did everything he could to try to make her happy. Unfortunately, Fran was never quite satisfied with Erik's offerings. She was often cold, aloof, and unresponsive to his many overtures of affection. One Christmas, Erik spent a lot of time deliberating over what to buy Fran as a gift. He went to nearly a dozen stores and finally chose a red dress he knew would look beautiful on her. He watched with eager anticipation on Christmas morning while she opened the gift, hoping that she would be as pleased with the dress as he was. As she lifted the dress out of its box he knew by the look on her face that he had failed again. Although Fran politely thanked him, Erik knew that she would be returning the dress. As she placed the cover on the box, he asked if she was even going to try it on. "It's just not my style," she said coldly.

Erik was hurt. The event was a microcosm of their marriage: Erik giving the very best he had and Fran expecting him to know what she wanted, then judging him as failing to suit her expectations. Less than a month later, Erik asked Fran for a divorce. She was shocked. Although Fran suspected that sooner or later they would divorce, she never thought that Erik would be the one to initiate it. This hit her hard and provoked a process of painful self-examination that eventually led her to see how her impossible expectations had set up the marriage for disaster.

Erik went on to marry someone else by whom he felt appreciated. Over time, Fran came to understand and regret the pain she had inflicted on Erik through her inflated image of herself. She learned a hard lesson through the loss of her marriage. The red dress became a symbol in her future relationships that reminded her to not lapse into her old sense of entitlement. Fran gradually relinquished her throne of superiority, and she eventually remarried. She became a kinder and more generous person in her second marriage. She learned the real meaning of the word "humility" and found that it didn't require a sacrifice of her personal power or self-respect. She learned that it wasn't wise to look to her marriage to make her happy, but rather to use her relationship to become a more loving and fulfilled person.

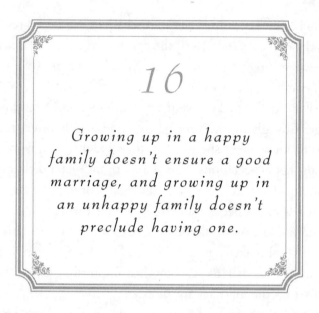

16

Growing up in a happy family doesn't ensure a good marriage, and growing up in an unhappy family doesn't preclude having one.

LINDA: I have a friend named Sally. She is one of those uncommon people who grew up in a secure, loving, happy family. Her parents loved each other dearly. They were devoted to her, giving her enough structure to promote feelings of security and enough freedom to explore and investigate the world. Her grandmother lived with the family and was also very caring. There was no yelling, and everyone talked things over when decisions needed to be made. As a little girl, Sally grew up lavished by the love of three adoring adults. Before I met Sally I hadn't known a single person who came from such a family. I assumed that if you grew up in such idyllic circumstances, you would live a harmonious life and a happy marriage would be guaranteed. This is not so. Although Sally does have a happy marriage now, there were many rough spots in getting there, not the least of which was her inability to fight and to draw boundaries. As a child she never had to.

Unlike Sally's, my childhood was less than ideal. I came into marriage fearing that my background would limit my ability to create the kind of life with Charlie that I really wanted. I was envious of those who I believed were blessed to have grown up in a happy family. However, I came to realize that although they have a definite advantage in knowing what a happy marriage looks and feels like, they still have their work to do, just like the rest of us. Most of us come from families that are less than perfect, to say the least. Our parents, like their parents before them, were limited in their ability to provide unconditional love, leaving us with wounds and disappointments that we bring to our adult relationships.

These hurts needn't limit our ability to love. In fact, they can be the means by which we develop greater compassion and sensitivity toward others and ourselves. In time, we come to understand that our past experiences do not necessarily limit our capacity to give and receive love. Instead, our potential to love can deepen as we come to meet, embrace, and learn from our painful experiences. The wounds themselves become the teachers, as we recover the ability to keep our hearts open. When we work with them in a gentle, caring, wise way, old hurts become the very doorway to loving more richly than we might ever have imagined.

17

*It's never too late
to repair damaged trust.*

There is no statute of limitations regarding hurt feelings or wounded trust. The bad news is that the pain of unfinished business can continue for years; the good news is that it's never too late to heal old wounds, even if they happened long ago.

Rose was sixty-nine and Harry was seventy-eight when he suffered a serious heart attack. For nearly two years, Rose devoted herself to Harry's recovery. They both agreed that her devoted care literally saved his life. However, in the process of being Harry's caretaker, Rose had overextended herself and was suffering from "compassion fatigue." Shortly after Harry's recovery, Rose fell into ill health and became depressed. She and Harry had been partners in a success-ful business, and now they were facing the possibility of losing it due to their deteriorating health. Not yet ready to transition into retirement, they both kept struggling to save the business, despite Rose's unhappiness, exhaustion, and growing resentment.

Harry welcomed the opportunity to reciprocate Rose's devotion, and he threw himself into caring for her as his strength slowly returned. Things, however, did not go according to plan. Rose didn't trust the depth of Harry's feelings for her. She feared that if she really needed him, he wouldn't be there for her. As a result, Harry often felt that in Rose's eyes he couldn't do anything right, and he was frustrated that his efforts didn't succeed in making her happy. Rose acknowledged that they had never created a foundation of deep intimacy in their marriage, and she feared it was too late. Together, they decided to seek couple counseling. Harry learned to be more responsive to Rose and more patient with himself. Rather than argue with her, which had fueled a power struggle, he committed himself to demonstrating his love and gratitude, regardless of how it might be received. As a way of showing his love, Harry came every week to either couple or individual therapy sessions. He also shopped, cooked, and told Rose that he loved her each day. He searched for prospective buyers for their business, took her to Hawaii, listened patiently to her distress, and became less reactive to her outbursts and criticisms. He even cooked chicken soup for the first time in his life!

Harry and Rose had not had an active sex life for six years. His snoring and tossing and turning had led them to sleep in separate rooms. They agreed to try a ritual of lying down beside each other in bed to be close before going to their separate rooms. Gradually, a feeling of kindness and gentleness came back into their marriage. Over the months, their intimacy grew. Rose eventually accepted Harry's efforts and softened into her love for him. The months of focused attention to their relationship paid off with a sweetness and trust greater than anything they had previously known. In their sunset years, they developed the love they had always longed for.

18

Secrets are lies.

Angela wanted to marry Ted so badly that she agreed with his request to not have children. In her heart, however, she cherished the hope that she could get him to change his mind. Eight years into the marriage, Ted discovered that Angela had contracted with a sperm bank. She had spent several thousand dollars, over eighteen months, trying to become pregnant. One day, when a bill showed up at home, Ted wondered, "What's this?" and asked Angela about it. Unable to continue her concealment and uneasy with the deceit, Angela finally admitted the truth. Ted was incredulous. "I can't believe you deceived me! How could you lie to me this way?"

Angela insisted, "I never lied. I just didn't tell you what I was doing. It was like a secret."

"You lied to me!" Ted shouted. "And you lied to me when you said you didn't want children."

"That isn't true," Angela said. "I really thought I wouldn't mind not having children, but then my feelings changed and I was afraid to tell you. I was afraid you wouldn't understand and would not budge on your original decision."

"And so you also lied to me when you changed your mind," Ted said.

"No, I just never told you. That was a secret too."

Not surprisingly, Ted and Angela didn't make it, not just because of the child issue, but because this example was only one in a larger pattern that included many instances of withholding. Both of them were rationalizing that the other wouldn't understand or that discussing things might make things worse. The most damaging rationale of all was the belief that these weren't lies but simply omissions, which could somehow be more easily excused.

Any deliberate attempt to misrepresent how we feel or what we've done is damaging to a relationship. Whether we call it a lie or a secret is irrelevant. What matters is the intention; when the intention is to create a misleading impression, even when the desire is to "protect" our partner, the result upon discovery will always be diminished trust. Marriage requires as high a standard of integrity as any commitment in our lives. Putting an end to secrecy does not require us to give up our right to privacy, and when we commit ourselves to this high standard of integrity, our relationship will thrive.

19

*Sex can improve
with age.*

One of the most common complaints we hear from couples is that their sex life has become stale, and the fire that used to ignite their passions has dimmed or even gone out entirely. Although sexual satisfaction does diminish for some couples over time, this is not inevitable. For many couples, the factors that most strongly impact the quality of their sexual experience are their expectations and the degree of trust in the relationship. We believe that the three most frequent contributors to a diminished sex life are 1) the belief that it is inevitable, 2) a lessening or loss of trust due to unresolved or unexpressed feelings between the partners, and 3) the tendency to hold the other person responsible for the sexual vitality of the relationship. When couples complain that "the spark has gone out of our marriage," it's generally because of one or more of the above conditions. The real problem often has to do with defensive mind states that limit authentic relatedness. It's more a "hardening of the attitudes" than a softening of the anatomy.

For many couples, sex actually improves over time. While the sexual experience may lose some of the fire and intensity of the early days of infatuation, it can become sweeter, richer, and more sensually delightful. As we get to know each other's minds, bodies, and souls more intimately, we become more able to respond in ways that are not only physically stimulating, but also emotionally and spiritually enriching. As we age and deepen from our life experiences, we may see that we are more than our aging bodies. We can enjoy the kind of relaxed and effortless connection that naturally arises when two people know each other completely. Anxiety over performance and self-consciousness melt away, and we can bathe in the delight of uninhibited sensory exploration. This kind of play and pleasuring encompasses more than the genitals or even the body; it extends to our whole being. This experience is only available when we have freed ourselves from the grip of limiting expectations. Deepened trust and intimacy through years of authentic relatedness expand our capacity for joy through shared experience. When both partners support each other's growth, the sexual connection will never become flat or boring. As our capacity to live life more fully increases, so does our ability to connect to each other, not only sexually, but in every other way as well.

20

*If you're keeping pace with
the people around you,
you're probably
moving too fast.*

LINDA: For much of my life, I lived as though more was good, and faster was better. Now I am a recovering rushaholic, and life is much sweeter, although the change hasn't been easy. When I would want to linger in the bed in the morning, to snuggle before jumping up to start the day; I would often meet with resistance from Charlie, as well as my rushaholic self. The taskmaster inside my mind would be yelling, "Get up, don't waste time, there is work to be done, don't be lazy!" When I would want to go to bed early and unwind after a hectic day, my inner critic would accuse me of weakness and insist that I push myself to be productive until late at night. I would cram countless activities, conversations, appointments, phone calls, and errands into each day. Everyone around me seemed to be dashing as fast or faster, competing as hard or harder, and we were all breathless.

Then one day I got the shocking news that I had cancer, and overnight everything changed. There is nothing like a life-threatening illness to force one to put things in perspective. Suddenly all those things that had been so important seemed trivial. Filling my life with activities that kept me moving nonstop throughout the day no longer made sense. My priorities drastically changed as I lost much of the motivation that had driven me to accomplish and achieve. I stopped being a "human doing" and started living like a "human being," more aware of what mattered to me, of what my heart truly desired.

One of the first things I noticed was a longing for more intimacy with Charlie, and a feeling of sadness over not having it. Even though we had been spending more time together in recent years, the truth was that I wanted even more but had felt that I was being greedy. Cancer changed that! Charlie and I began carving out intimacy time more frequently than ever before, from tiny micro-breaks during our workdays to weekend retreats together and vacations without the kids — which was something we had rarely done before. I stopped racing; I hired people to work with me, and I did whatever I needed to do to slow down.

I discovered that while life in the fast lane may be exciting and stimulating, it does not necessarily promote loving and intimate relationships. The mind travels at a faster speed than the heart. The connection that we seek with our beloved requires a slower velocity. Thus, if we want or need to slow down, we must be willing to experience the anxiety and impatience that often accompanies such a change of pace. Slowing down, quieting down, and paying closer attention to our own feelings and needs, as well as those of our partner, will do more to restore health and well-being to our lives and our relationships than anything else we can do. While it may take a while to break the habit of "rushaholism," once it is broken, our lives are permanently and positively transformed.

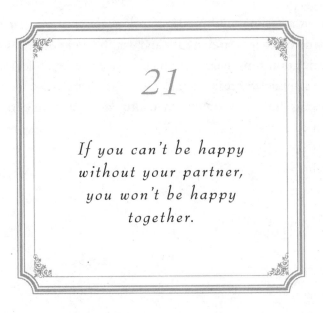

21

If you can't be happy
without your partner,
you won't be happy
together.

CHARLIE: When it comes down to it, we marry for one reason: we think that we'll be happier than we would be being single. Human beings crave happiness and will do whatever we think will bring more of it into our lives. I married Linda because I felt better with her in my life and believed that if we stayed together we could create even more happiness. We seemed to be good for each other. In reality, both Linda and I were young and immature, and neither of us was willing to really try to find out why we didn't have our desired level of happiness in our lives to begin with. We knew that life was better, easier, and less lonely when we were with each other... except when it wasn't. At those times, we each assumed that it was because the other was selfishly withholding whatever it was that we wanted at the time — intimacy, appreciation, sex, attention, or understanding. Or we felt that the other was giving too much of what we didn't want — advice, criticism, control, judgment, resentment, disappointment, or distance.

It wasn't until we were well into our marriage that it became clear to us that our individual happiness was up to each of us. As long as we held the other person responsible for providing fulfillment, there would be no end to blame, resentment, and self-pity. There's a huge difference between enjoying the happiness that our partner brings into our life and on the other hand seeing it as their job to make us happy. Unfortunately, too many of us enter into marriage believing that we will magically be redeemed from the unhappiness of feeling unloved, unworthy, lonely, insecure, or depressed. The belief that "love heals all wounds" is still disturbingly pervasive in our culture, and it is a myth that needs a proper burial.

When your happiness requires something from another person, what you have isn't love; it's codependence. Country music standards notwithstanding, real love isn't about being "so lonesome I could die" or being "nothing without you" or feeling that "you're my world, you're my everything." This may be the stuff of romantic ballads, but in practice it's a surefire prescription for excessive dependence, which fosters control, resentment, and unhappiness. The more capable you are of creating inner happiness, otherwise known as joy, the happier you will be with another person.

When we take responsibility for healing the unloved places within ourselves by accepting and internalizing our partner's love, true healing and happiness begins. Paradoxically, though we may not become truly happy without someone else's love, their love alone is not enough to fulfill us. What their love can do is to ignite the spark of self-love buried deep in our hearts so that we can recognize, feed, and nurture it until it becomes a roaring fire that ultimately burns up the shame, insecurity, anger, and pain that have been the sources of our unhappiness. When two individuals interact in this way, they can experience a depth of joy beyond what either had imagined.

22

Marriage is like yoga.

LINDA: Hatha yoga, the physical aspect of an Indian spiritual system, is becoming popular throughout the Western world. It consists of postures, or asanas, that involve stretching our muscles, as well as attention to our breath and meditation practices. As a longtime yoga practitioner, I've discovered that the principles of yoga can be applied to marriage. Just as the regular practice of yoga leads to a strong, attractive, healthy body, the regular practice of relationship yoga leads to a strong, beautiful marriage.

We develop strength and flexibility by stretching into our partner's world. Because we tend to be attracted to people who are in many ways different from ourselves, relationships provide ever-present opportunities to practice stretching — opening ourselves up to and accepting feelings, behaviors, tastes, preferences, and values that may be very different from those with which we are familiar and comfortable.

Intimate connection requires stretching to the point of distress. The challenge is not to avoid the discomfort, but to stay with it to better understand ourselves as well as our partner. As in yoga, we must hold the stretch to become more adept in staying with the discomfort, but we need to know ourselves well enough to recognize when to ease up so as not to risk injury. Over-stretching can be harmful, but if we ease up too soon, we'll never grow stronger. By finding this exquisite balance point, we get the most out of our yoga and our marriage.

As our yoga practice grows, we develop the capacity to tolerate increasing levels of discomfort while remaining still in difficult postures. This stretching allows us to develop tone. It's the same in marriage. We gradually become more acclimated to positions that we had previously found to be highly uncomfortable. This is not a matter of accepting an intolerable situation such as abuse or disrespect, but rather of increasing our levels of personal strength, openness, flexibility, and acceptance. We stay present with our own feelings of sadness, anger, or fear. When we welcome and gently embrace these feelings, we can stay connected to our partner with an open, caring heart. We can even move into positions we never imagined we could tolerate, and we are pleasantly surprised to discover that we can find balance there.

Hatha means force; *yoga* means union. The force results from the joining of *ha,* which means sun, and *tha,* which means moon. In many spiritual traditions, the sun is associated with the masculine, the moon with the feminine. The practice of joining the masculine and feminine in a balanced way results in a powerful force. When we practice the postures in yoga, the inner masculine and feminine come into balance, resulting in a supple, graceful body. When we use our marriage as a practice, the inner masculine and feminine come into balance as well. Instead of resisting the masculine active, initiatory, competitive, penetrating, assertive principles, we learn to honor these energies; instead of denigrating the feminine receptive, passive, sensitive, yielding, patient principles, we come to respect and appreciate them. If the sun and moon within each individual can coexist in harmony, then the energies of two individuals can blend to manifest as a graceful, supple partnership.

In yoga, regular practice leads to greater proficiency, and long-term daily practice allows us to excel at the art. So it is with relationship yoga; the consistent practice of handling differences with generosity and goodwill serves to strengthen both the individuals as well as the relationship itself.

One of the goals of the yoga practice is to become physically healthy by stimulating all the body's systems — respiratory, circulatory, muscular, skeletal, digestive, eliminatory, and reproductive. We practice to enhance our energy, to remain youthful and vital into old age, and to live a long, productive life. These same benefits are available to those who adopt relationship yoga as their practice. As recent scientific evidence shows, those in good marriages suffer fewer diseases and live longer. Through contemplation, devotion, and action, yoga practitioners experience both ecstatic states as well as peace of mind; by being considerate and active in their devotion, marital partners, too, can experience ecstatic states as well as a profound quality of inner peace.

23

The prince isn't going to come.

Holly grew up with a father who doted on her and her mother. She worshipped and idealized him and lived in luxury and comfort. She found it easy to believe in fairy tales that ended in "happily ever after." When she got married, she was shocked to discover that her husband actually had flaws. Holly suffered for months with unhappiness. She was certain that she had married the wrong man. She fantasized that if she had married a different kind of man, more like her father, she would have continued to live a charmed life. When she wasn't being resentful of her husband's shortcomings, she was blaming herself for being a terrible, ungrateful wife. She found herself depressed, and eventually she entered into therapy. Holly's therapist attempted to help her be more realistic in her expectations of married life and to investigate choices that would bring her more satisfaction. With help, a more realistic side of Holly was evolving. Still, the childlike romantic did not want to give up her dreams.

One day Holly literally awoke to the realization that her dreams and expectations were empty of substance and built on childish hopes and fears. Sobbing, she called her therapist. "I've been betrayed," she said. "Why didn't anyone tell me the truth? All the fairy stories are sheer fantasy. No one is going to take care of me. I feel like such a fool for believing all that crap. Everything I believed in is wrong." It was a painful but powerful awakening.

Holly committed herself to the process of learning how to take care of herself emotionally, physically, and financially. In time, she opened her own business and became a successful entrepreneur. She managed to create a wholesome marriage as well. This new marriage was with her husband, the same man she had once found to be a disappointment. Now she was able to accept him with his flaws and humanness.

Some women realize their prince isn't going to come during the course of their marriage, some during a painful divorce. Sadly, some women move into midlife lonely, still waiting. Romantic myths are slow to die. Some stubborn part of us wants desperately to believe that there is someone out there who will gratify every desire and bring us happiness, ease, and peace. Nowadays, Holly still loves fairy stories, but her favorites are the ones with wicked witches and dumb giants. She makes a point of telling the young women in her life to pay attention to the imagery of the dark side, because that's part of life too.

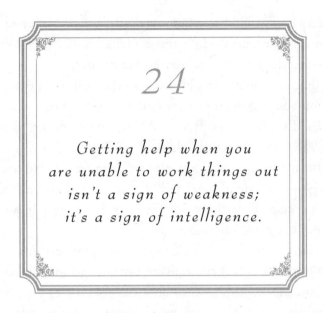

24

Getting help when you are unable to work things out isn't a sign of weakness; it's a sign of intelligence.

LINDA: Most couples wait too long to get help. Unnecessary suffering occurs in secrecy and isolation when you are too embarrassed to ask for assistance. The time to get help for your marriage is when one (not both) of you feels the need for it. Putting this agreement in place before things deteriorate will support early intervention and prevent painful, time-consuming arguments later on.

I once heard Malidoma Somé, a healer and ritualist, tell a story about his homeland in Africa. He is of the Dagara tribe in Burkino, West Africa. In this community everyone understands that the well-being of the entire tribe depends on the success of each married couple. The whole tribe supports the couple. If a woman attempts to communicate something important to her husband and he is unresponsive, she goes to her women friends. At first they advise her, and if her husband doesn't respond, they speak to him directly. By then he is usually motivated to take action, because if things don't work out after he speaks with the women, his wife's next recourse is to approach the other men in the tribe. Generally, the husband recoils at the prospect of being confronted by his male peers! Of course, it works both ways. The husband has the same system of support available if his wife is closed to something that is important to him. First he will approach the men for advice, then his men friends may meet face to face with his wife. As a last resort, he will turn to the tribal women.

For many in our culture, this tradition seems a terrible invasion of privacy. But I see great wisdom in this high level of community support. I can remember numerous times when I wanted desperately to reach Charlie and was frustrated in not being able to do so. I'm sure we wouldn't have gotten so stuck if we had had a system in place that allowed for the influence of family and friends. While their advice may not always be helpful, we all need the love and companionship of our friends, even when things are moving along well. We especially need their support when the inevitable stresses and challenges of life occur. Somé says that in our American culture, the couple begins at the top of the mountain and falls off. In his tribe, the couple starts at the bottom of the mountain, and the whole community pushes the couple to the top. It is the wise couple who solicits assistance from family, friends, and professionals. All of us have blind spots and, at times, can benefit from objective input and feedback. When life knocks us down, our loved ones can help us to climb back up.

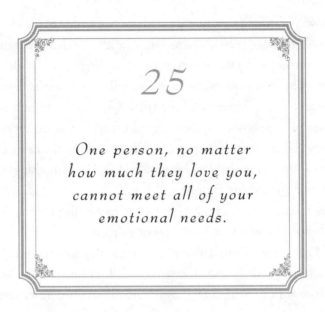

25

*One person, no matter
how much they love you,
cannot meet all of your
emotional needs.*

Another popular myth about marriage is that if someone loves us fully, purely, and unconditionally, we shouldn't need anyone else's love and support. This mistaken notion has been the source of great suffering, disappointment, and disillusionment for many couples. While marriage can be delightful, healing, challenging, and stimulating, it is sheer fantasy to believe that this relationship alone can fulfill us. We also need friends, satisfying work, healthy solitude, play, and other life experiences to fulfill the needs of our soul. Unrealistic expectations inevitably set us up for disappointment.

While there is only one word for "love" in the English language, there are over three hundred words describing different types of love in Pali, the language of ancient Buddhism, and seventy-six in Persian. How many kinds of love are there? For starters, there are parental love, filial love, platonic love, the constant love of a friend, the love of beauty, the fiery love of a new romance, and the deep and enduring love of a long-standing marriage. One person cannot possibly love us in all of the ways we need to be loved. Relieving our partner and ourselves from the obligation to provide for the full range of our love needs brings a truer, stronger, and more sustaining quality of love into our relationship.

The many varieties of love fulfill many different needs within us. A need is anything that is essential to our health and well-being. Some needs we can meet within ourselves, some can only be met in intimate relationships or committed partnerships, some through other relationships. If we believe that we can or should be all things for our partner and vice versa, the relationship is probably headed for disaster. That's an impossible burden that no single individual can fulfill, and the expectation itself sets us up for disappointment and failure. This expectation may be a thin disguise for the desire to possess and control the other person, a manipulative strategy that stems from a feeling of insecurity or unworthiness within us. As we become more affirming of our own essential worth and lovability, we no longer need to limit the people with whom we share our love.

The more secure we feel within ourselves, the more able we are to grant our partner the room they need to include other loving relationships into their life. Offering this generosity of spirit and the underlying trust that it demonstrates is likely to make us more attractive to our partner and make them appreciate us more. This gratitude recycles back to them, as we appreciate their appreciation and feel affirmed as worthy and loving beings. Thus we complete a self-affirming, positive cycle that replaces the vicious cycle of mistrust that may have previously been operating. Although such transformations may seem unlikely, we are living proof that they are possible and without question worth the time and effort they require.

26

Love isn't always enough to sustain a marriage.

Couples can usually resolve or work out personality differences and make room for these differences to coexist. There are, however, some differences that are true dealbreakers. Different sexual orientations, desires to have or not have children, and serious value differences regarding such issues as honesty or monogamy can mean the end of a marriage.

Serafina and Mica were married with two boys, one in nursery school and the other in first grade. Serafina was very much in love with Mica, but over time, she felt increasingly that he was not reciprocating her affections. When she expressed her concerns to Mica, he denied feeling disinterested in her, but Serafina remained unconvinced. She fretted over what she could do to make herself more attractive to him, but nothing she tried seemed to work.

Finally, Mica revealed to her that he had experienced several homosexual liaisons during the course of their marriage. Serafina was devastated. She had never suspected that her husband was gay. She had always assumed that he didn't find her sexy or didn't love her. Mica told her that he had withheld the truth because he was terrified of how she might respond to it and how it would damage their family. He knew that his whole life would change in the instant he revealed his burdensome secret. Normally a compassionate person, Serafina was beyond her capacity for understanding. She was incensed by the lies and deceit that had been going on for years and furious that Mica had exposed her to serious health risks.

They both agreed that this was not a marriage that could or should be saved, and they agreed to go their separate ways. Mica soon came out of the closet to the rest of his family and close friends. Serafina and Mica engaged in conversations attempting to heal their damaged relationship so that they could parent their two boys together. She came to understand that Mica was not at fault for being homosexual, accepting that he had no choice about his sexual orientation. She also understood that at the time they married he had not allowed himself to recognize his true sexual orientation. Out of their many discussions, she came to appreciate the terror he had been feeling about telling people the truth in a society that still holds so much prejudice.

Mica continued to be a devoted father to his two sons.

After a period of emotional recovery for both Serafina and Mica, they were able to cultivate a friendship that supports them to this day. In fact, like many couples who resolve their deeper differences after the dissolution of their marriage, they have become much better friends now than they were when they were married.

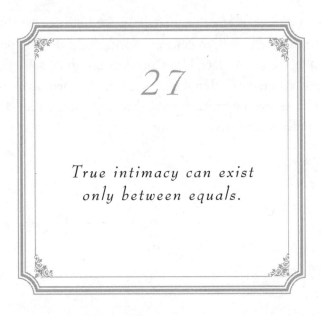

*True intimacy can exist
only between equals.*

Melony and Jude married when they were both barely out of their teens. Like many couples, neither of them had experienced or observed much genuine intimacy in their lives or families prior to meeting and marrying. Melony's mother was a hyper-responsible super-mom who worked full time, did the shopping, cooking, and cleaning, managed the money, helped the children with homework, and volunteered at church in her spare time. Melony grew up believing that this was what a good wife and mother was supposed to do. Trying to live up to these impossible expectations frequently left her exhausted, depleted, and resentful. She often felt stressed out and anxious.

Her husband, Jude, had a completely different temperament. He was relaxed to the point of being irresponsible at times and had much lower standards of order and control in his life. Melony treated Jude like one of the kids. Sometimes he complied with her frequent requests and demands, and sometimes he didn't. Although Jude claimed that he didn't mind Melony's constant reminders, too often he felt resentful, and his feelings periodically leaked out. In the meantime, she was feeling increasingly angry for "having to" do so much work herself.

Predictably, a time came when Jude and Melony could no longer contain these feelings. Things came to a head when Jude initiated an affair with one of Melony's closest friends. To say that Melony was upset when she got the news from her friend would be a huge understatement. In her opinion, a slow, agonizing death for both Jude and her friend would have been an inadequate consequence for the crime. Her first response was to throw Jude out of the house. Things went downhill from there.

Unaccustomed to life in a cheap motel and never having lived on his own, Jude was not particularly pleased with the latest turn of events. He had vastly underestimated Melony's willingness to live without him. Determined to win her back, Jude appealed to her for a second chance. "No way," she insisted. He begged, pleaded, apologized, and promised to never do it again. Slowly, Melony's resistance softened; after three months she consented to enter marriage counseling. Gradually they were able to see how they had colluded to create an environment that had culminated in Jude's affair. It became obvious to them both how the roles of the misbehaving boy and the controlling mother had predisposed their marriage to disaster. They took on the task of rebuilding the structure of their relationship in a way that created a greater degree of equality and shared responsibility.

They were able to pull back from the edge of the abyss just in time. During the course of therapy, Melony saw that by taking a position of power and control, handling decisions with no collaboration with Jude, she had precluded him from being a true and equal partner. Jude had thought that he was getting off easy by not having to be attentive to the children and the house. He had no idea of the price he was paying for being detached from the ongoing requirements of running a family and household.

During the time that they lived apart, Jude experienced a crash course in how to be an adult. For the first time in his life he was responsible for shopping, cooking, cleaning, managing money, and, when he had visitation, actively participating in the raising of his children. Over time, his aptitude for responsibility grew, along with his self-esteem. Melony noticed his increased competence and began to relate to him with more respect, her resentment gradually melting away. She began to trust that he actually did care deeply for her, and she felt his love manifested in his actions, which reflected his consideration for her.

For Melony, the searing pain of the sexual betrayal began to fade. Eventually, she was able to forgive Jude, and they began to truly share decision-making for the first time. They discovered a level of intimacy that they had never before experienced. They moved back in together with a new vow: to be equals in all ways.

When a couple is still playing out their struggle for power there are only intermittent flashes of intimacy; it is illusive and inconsistent. The desire to stay safe, be in control, and dominate undermines sustained intimacy. As long as the domination and submission cycle continues there can be no possibility of genuine closeness. As we continue to recognize even the most subtle ways we grasp for power, we can work skillfully with this protective tendency, and the quality of intimacy deepens.

The barriers to intimate connection crumble away when there are feelings of trust, safety, and respect. This attitude creates the grounding from which equality flows very naturally. As we recognize the triggers that stimulate old patterns of self-protection, we can address and systematically disarm them, both internally and in dialogue with our partner.

Like a skilled technician who steps cautiously into a minefield to deactivate the bombs, it takes great courage to do this tedious and dangerous work. Our reward is the joy that comes in playing and dancing together with abandon and delight, as equals.

28

*The real issue is
usually not the one
you're arguing about.*

Jim and Vivian saw eye to eye on almost everything, but there was one area where their differences were irreconcilable. Jim smoked pot and Vivian strongly disapproved. Not only did he smoke it, but unbeknownst to Vivian he also grew it. That is, until the day she discovered a rather large marijuana plant in the midst of her precious sunflowers. She went wild. "Are you out of your mind? What are you thinking? We could get arrested! My career could be ruined! How could you do this?"

Although Jim thought that Vivian was exaggerating the risk, he sensed that it might not be a good idea to provoke her any further and agreed to destroy the pot plants. But he couldn't quite bring himself to destroy *all* of the plants, so he moved a few to a section of their spacious yard that he thought would escape his wife's scrutiny. He was wrong. The uproar when Vivian discovered the newly transplanted pot plants could be heard throughout the neighborhood. Jim considered moving into a motel for a while but then reconsidered and decided to once again (gulp) face his wife's wrath.

She raged and he listened without arguing, justifying, or defending himself. He just let her express all of her anger and hurt until she had nothing left to say. Then a strange thing happened. Vivian started to cry. Underneath all of her anger was the fear that this difference might be so important that it would destroy their marriage. She cried out of the fear that they would not make it. Seeing how much pain Vivian was in made Jim cry as well. He could see that she didn't hate him, but that she was feeling that he didn't care enough about her concerns to give up growing the plants. "That's ridiculous! I wouldn't trade our marriage for all the pot in the world!" When he really listened, he understood, for the first time, the real issue. At that moment, their marriage was transformed.

In this case, as in many, drugs were the symptom, not the source of the problem. Jim not only stopped growing pot in his backyard, but he stopped smoking it as well — not because Vivian insisted upon it, but because he saw that his smoke-saturated mind had trouble understanding and relating to his beloved partner. The real issue was not about drugs. It was about caring enough to listen deeply and respond from the loving truth of the heart.

29

Love isn't just a feeling;
it's an action that shows
our caring.

CHARLIE: As a marriage counselor and seminar leader, I hear many intimate details of the lives of my clients and students. Partners often complain to each other that they feel unloved. This statement frequently triggers a strong reaction, the accused trying to convince their partner of their love, perhaps expressing disbelief or even outrage that there can be any question about it. They might insist that their love is real and strong and even infer that there must be something wrong with their partner for expressing such a complaint. While it may be true that the accused does in fact feel great love toward their partner, it may be equally true that this love is not being expressed or received in a way that leads to a feeling of appreciation and value.

One of the recurring arguments in my own marriage

revolved around this complaint. Whenever Linda would tell me that she felt lonely, disconnected, or unloved, I would immediately attempt to convince her that she was wrong to feel that way. Invariably I would trot out all kinds of evidence that I used as "proof" that her feelings were invalid. Not surprisingly, this strategy didn't do a lot to make Linda feel loved or listened to. What she really wanted from me wasn't proof of my love. She wanted loving action — in this case, me listening openly, respectfully, and nonreactively to her feelings, without trying to make her wrong and me right.

If our love does not show up in our actions, it isn't really love. This doesn't mean that we don't love our partner, only that at times our willingness or ability to show it is obscured by a conflicting commitment (such as wanting to protect ourselves, be right, avoid conflict, et cetera) that is getting in the way. If you really intend to be a world-class lover, then you have to learn to show it regularly and frequently in countless ways. In the best relationships, both partners know each other in such intimate detail that they know the things that fill each other's love tank. In addition, they have cultivated and deepened a spirit of generosity that spills over to all aspects of their lives. The sincere expression of love given freely, resonating and reverberating back and forth, gives rise to the exquisite beauty of deep relatedness.

30

*Expectations set us up
for resentment.*

LINDA: If you can't do something without expecting something in return, you're probably better off not doing it at all. A marriage is not a business deal. Keeping score may work in sports and finances, but it's folly in a relationship. Rather than keeping track of whether or not the ledger is balanced, work instead to cultivate trust and a spirit of goodwill. That which is given from a selfless intention is always rewarded.

As a psychotherapist, I know that Valentine's Day, wedding anniversaries, birthdays, Mother's Day, Father's Day, vacations, Christmas, and New Year's Eve are high-risk times for marital disappointment. People who don't get what they expect — be it flowers, candy, romantic greeting cards, or sex — often find themselves hurt and angry. One woman I know was so enraged at her husband's "neglect" that she threw the card he had given her in his face. He retaliated by ripping it up. Happy Valentine's Day.

During the Christmas season, other responses are predictable. One of my clients welcomed the New Year by weeping in her car alone. She felt slighted and ignored when her husband failed to pay her what she considered to be sufficient attention at a holiday party. Instead of expressing her feelings to him, she was so upset that she stalked away from the party alone.

We all have expectations; it's only natural. But if we can't loosen our white-knuckle grip on how we think things are supposed to be, we're setting ourselves up for great and frequent disappointment. Instead of getting attached to an idealized vision of an upcoming event, we can ask ourselves the question, "What's the experience I want to have?" This question provides spaciousness around the relationship so it's not so tight and cramped. Then, together with our partner, we can create what we want our special occasion to look and feel like.

The ability to create special occasions for our partner and with our partner that are truly gratifying is a skill that can be perfected over time. The process itself can be disappointing because things don't always go according to plan, regardless of how hard we try. It's not so much a matter of avoiding disappointments as it is learning to accept their inevitability and deal with them without blame, resentment, or retaliation when they occur. In a workshop, the famous family therapist James Framo once said, "Give up all the expectations except the ones you are willing to die for." While that may seem a bit dramatic, it's actually pretty good advice.

31

Arguments can't be avoided,
but destructive ones can.

Loving someone doesn't mean never disagreeing with them, and it doesn't mean that settling conflicts with them is easy. Differences are not only inevitable, they are a significant part of what makes us attractive to each other. And they don't disappear when you love someone. In fact, they often become more pronounced. The more secure we feel in the relationship, the more free we feel to express difficult emotions and desires and voice powerful truths. Marriages with the deepest level of intimacy are often those in which divergent views, feelings, and opinions are most openly expressed and received. These couples deal with differences in ways that promote greater truthfulness, trust, and respect. Avoiding the honest expression of differences in a relationship often causes more damage than would a clearly spoken feeling of resentment or disappointment.

We don't necessarily need to fight, and we certainly don't need to insist on getting our way, but we do need to know that we can and will stand up for ourselves by speaking our truth, listening nondefensively, and taking appropriate and responsible action when necessary. To fail to protect oneself in the face of an attack is as irresponsible as neglecting a child. Taking a stand in the face of danger requires courage and discernment. It means restraining ourselves from unnecessarily punitive reactions and limiting our responses to those that are kind and constructive, rather than those that are offensive and destructive. No matter how deeply we love someone, strong or hurtful words may slip out, especially when we're feeling tired, stressed, or upset. Rather than withholding their differences, the best-functioning couples are the ones who have mastered "conscious combat." They are skilled warriors of the heart. Skillful action not only helps us move through difficult situations more quickly, it helps us use each breakdown as a means of deepening trust and understanding.

32

*One of the greatest gifts
we can give our partner is
our focused attention.*

Belle and Dutch never seemed to be able to match their schedules. She went to bed after dinner; he stayed up and read. He leapt out of bed at 6 A.M. to head for the gym; she slept until 7. His idea of a good time was sitting in front of the computer or working on projects in his garage workshop; hers was snuggling on the sofa. Dutch liked to constantly be doing something, while Belle preferred to connect and just hang out together.

Belle was an appreciative wife, praising Dutch's work on their house, but she experienced a growing sense of frustration because they weren't connecting. Sometimes she would be assertive, saying, "Come be with me." Dutch often responded defensively, "What are you talking about? I'm right here." But even as he was responding, Dutch was lying on his back in the bed looking at the ceiling, not touching Belle, barely hearing her, deep inside himself, lost in his own thoughts. They were in the same vicinity, but not emotionally close. One of the things getting in the way was that Dutch heard Belle's requests as complaints about his adequacy, and he felt judged and scolded by her, even though that was not Belle's intention. In response, he would withdraw and become even more disengaged. They were in a vicious cycle.

One day Belle broke down, in tears not of frustration and anger but of sadness. She feared that they would not ever be able to connect the way she wanted to. While Belle was crying, Dutch was thinking, "Here we go again." But this time was different. The frustration that Dutch expected Belle to express did not come. Belle said, "I'm so scared that we're not going to be able to be with each other the way I want to be. I'm afraid we might not be able to get through this awful impasse. I really love you, but it hurts so much to feel so distant so much of the time." This got Dutch's attention, and for the first time he was able to feel what Belle was feeling and wanting without being defensive.

The depth of her feelings stunned Dutch. He couldn't think of anything to say. It was just the two of them together. Their shared fear and pain had finally been spoken and heard. In the silence, Dutch reached for Belle's hand and gently held it. Their eyes met. "Thanks," she said, "I needed that. Maybe it's not hopeless after all." The wordless gesture of reaching out his hand helped Dutch to understand what all of Belle's words couldn't convey to him. He started to realize what she wanted. Belle felt heard and met. She realized that two important things had prompted Dutch to respond to her this time: she was not irritable when she spoke to him, and she did not downplay the depth of her desire to be close. She was vulnerable, showing her fear and pain. This precedent proved to be a turning point in their relationship.

Belle and Dutch experienced increasingly more frequent openhearted connections, and the trust between them continued to grow. As Dutch became more familiar with the experience of openness, he began to feel more comfortable with his own vulnerability, and he could allow his boundaries to blur and defenses to drop with a kind of ease that he had never experienced. He became able to soften his tight grip on his defenses to listen more deeply to his partner. His focus shifted from protection to connection.

During this time, Belle was learning how to be more responsible and conscientious in identifying her own needs and getting them met. She saw that her work involved getting to know herself more intimately and that as she did so she was able to experience greater intimacy in her marriage. She also learned to manage the feelings, such as irritation and fear, that would arise when she desired more closeness with Dutch. Rather than approach him with anger and frustration, she learned to open her own heart before speaking with him, which increased the chances of a successful outcome.

If you talk to Dutch these days, he winks when he says, "If you have a happy wife, you have a happy life."

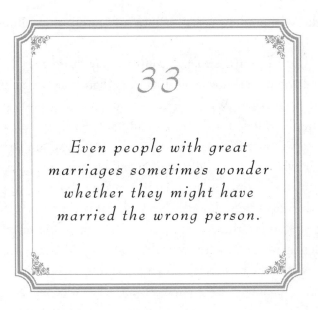

33

*Even people with great
marriages sometimes wonder
whether they might have
married the wrong person.*

CHARLIE: Temporary doubt isn't necessarily a reflection of something seriously wrong with the relationship. In a moment of anger or disappointment, disturbing thoughts can pop into anyone's head. The thoughts "This is not what I had in mind," "I made a mistake," or "I married too early" are based on the usually mistaken notion that somewhere there is a special someone with whom we would never argue, struggle, or feel disappointed, a soul mate with whom we would be spared all pain, suffering, and stress. Sadly, such dreams are the stuff of fantasy and rarely materialize in the lives of real people. Still, the hopes of perfect harmony die hard, and the fear of having made the wrong choice can shake us to the core. It's common for people to withhold these thoughts not only from others, but from themselves as well. Withholding tends to intensify rather than diminish doubt.

Until I joined a men's group I rarely heard my married male friends acknowledge that they had misgivings about their marriages. While there was plenty of grousing and grumbling, few of my friends admitted that they ever wondered whether they might have made a mistake in marrying their wives. I never admitted it either. Like the others, I assumed that since no one else was talking about this, I must be the only one feeling this way. The only time I ever heard anyone admit these feelings was after their marriage had fallen apart, and then it was often all I would hear.

When the members of my men's group, several of whom had solid, long-term marriages, all acknowledged periodic misgivings about their partners, I realized that these thoughts did not reflect bad marriages, but rather the truth of complex and dynamic normal committed partnerships. Wanting to collect a broader base for my informal research, I brought the question to other men and women in my life, particularly those who enjoyed what I considered to be successful relationships. The responses were nearly unanimous. Almost everyone had experienced questions about their choice of a partner, and most of them felt guilty thinking that they were the only one or that this was some form of disloyalty to the marriage. The honest acceptance of these kinds of occasional thoughts when they occur will strengthen rather than harm our marriages.

The challenge at these times is to determine whether these doubts are reflective of some deep flaw in our relationship or whether they are merely indicators of an underlying condition that temporarily requires our attention. In using these questions to enter into an internal inquiry, I usually uncover some unexpressed or unacknowledged feelings with which I need to come to terms, either by taking some action, communicating something I've been withholding, or simply letting go of something I cannot change. Chances are that I can do one of the above, and when I do, the doubt seems to dissolve or at least fade far enough into the background of my thoughts to allow my heart to open once again, in gratitude and appreciation for the woman I married.

34

*Your partner cannot rescue
you from unhappiness,
but they can help you
to rescue yourself.*

LINDA: When I picture myself as an eight-year-old, I see an only child, a lonely little girl, very serious and dreamy. I like to play house with the neighborhood kids so I can visualize being grown up, being the mommy and having a husband. In my imagined future, I am never lonely or frightened. It's embarrassing to admit how strongly the make-believe games and fairy tales I grew up with influenced me. I was actually waiting for Prince Charming to find Cinderella (me) and make a beautiful life for me. Inevitably, I brought this child-ish, unrealistic expectation into my marriage.

Everything was wonderful for about three weeks, and then came the crash (some honeymoon periods last longer than others). Marriage quickly cures the disease of naïveté.

In my case, it jarred me into the awareness that creating a life filled with happiness would require a supreme effort on my part, not just Charlie's.

Most of us tend to hold our partner responsible for our own happiness. This is, in fact, the driving motivation of many people for getting married. Left unchecked, however, these expectations can turn a perfectly good romance into a cauldron of smoldering resentment heated by the inevitable disappointment of unfulfilled expectations. We all come into marriage with longing, unhealed wounds, unmet needs, and other unfinished business that we secretly hope our beloved will heal.

It is undoubtedly a blessing to have some support and encouragement in this process. Although our partner can't remove our suffering or fulfill our deepest desires, there is an enormous amount that they can provide: they can be a vital force in our development; their caring, concern, and committed listening can all enhance our ability to find strength and courage; with their patient encouragement, we can experiment and test the waters of new possibility; when we lapse and falter, their steady belief in our eventual success gives us inspiration and a second wind; they can frequently see strengths and talents in us where we have blind spots and help us to recognize self-imposed obstacles that may be keeping us stuck. In building a loving connection together we learn to trust the caring of each other's feedback and learn to accept it with gratitude. Even the most difficult lessons can be a valuable resource in helping us to bring greater wholeness and happiness into our lives. While their love can provide a soothing balm to our own struggles, no one but ourselves can grant us true fulfillment. While it is certainly possible to recover from the pain of old wounds, ultimately it's an inside job.

35

The cost of a lie is far greater than any advantage you gain from speaking it.

CHARLIE: To be perfectly honest, I am not always perfectly honest. Trying to look good or impress others, I have been known to tell exaggerated stories about my accomplishments. This habit didn't instantly cease even after I decided to become a more honest person. While I rarely set out to be deliberately deceitful, at times old patterns get the best of me. Recently, I told Linda that I couldn't take one of our cats to the vet because I was not going to be free during the afternoon. Later that evening I had an uncomfortable feeling, which I traced back to our conversation. Although it was true that I was busy that day, I could have easily altered my schedule to bring Shadow to the cat doctor. Rather than tell the truth and admit that I'd just rather not do it, or mildly inconvenience myself to accommodate Linda's request, I fudged it. A little later, I sorted it out in my mind. I confessed to Linda, who thanked me for being honest and said that she had sensed something was off because I seemed edgy at dinner.

Lies, no matter how small, always take their toll on the trust, goodwill, and respect in our relationships. The bad news is that most of us are likely to struggle with issues of deceit throughout our lives. The good news is that as we practice being conscious communicators, we become aware and less tolerant of our own dishonesty. The further good news is that in cleaning up our own act, we inspire others to do the same.

Whether you call it a justification, a rationale, a white lie, a fib, a half-truth, or an exaggeration, a lie is a lie is a lie. What makes something a lie is the intention. We lie whenever we make a deliberate effort to mislead others to gain some advantage. Examples of advantages that I have tried to gain by lying to Linda in the past are: avoiding the possibility of conflict; creating a favorable impression with her; maintaining the upper hand; and wanting to prove that I was good, honorable, superior, intelligent, competent, successful, or some combination of the above. The underlying intention of most of my lies has to do with trying to influence the way Linda perceives me in order to maintain some degree of control in our relationship. It is an attempt to shape the relationship in accord with my own desires. To justify this somewhat unworthy intention, I have to create a set of rationalizations (basically, excuses for dishonesty).

The consequences of dishonesty are always the same: feelings of guilt and anxiety and an increased mistrust of self and others. We lie to avoid the unpleasant consequences of telling the truth. We don't want to look bad, feel bad, or upset others. Each time we use this form of avoidance we deepen our sense of being ill-equipped to handle the truth, thus reinforcing a feeling of inner weakness. This leads to further deceit. Lying undermines the foundation of a relationship more than anything else. Finding the courage and commitment to confront the tendency to lie can add strength, love, and integrity to our marriage. Although it isn't easy to break the habit of deceit, it is possible — even for those who have practiced subtle or not-so-subtle forms of it for years. The motivation for this work comes from seeing what we can gain by it. Setting foot on the path of integrity forever changes our lives for the better.

36

Even the best marriages have irreconcilable differences.

Flossy and Gabe were the kind of couple that made you wonder how on earth these two people ever found each other, much less stayed together. Flossy is a relentless doer, always involved with dozens of projects simultaneously. She rarely gets or needs more than three hours of sleep a night. When she wakes up, she's out of bed and on the move within seconds. Flossy is a conservative Republican who not so secretly hopes someday to enter and win a local election. She adheres to a firm and structured model of parenting that holds that too much freedom leaves kids feeling insecure and uncared for. She can talk for hours about issues related to psychology, spirituality, and human relations. When it comes to money, Flossy is frugal; "Waste not, want not" is her motto. Sports and business bore her to death; her attention span in those areas can be computed in seconds.

While Flossy is almost always on the move, Gabe's idea of a good time is sitting home and watching TV after dinner. He relishes sleep and can't function on less than nine hours. Politically, he's a liberal Democrat. As a parent, Gabe is easygoing and laissez-faire, believing that freedom helps kids to develop self-responsibility, and that excessive structure fosters unhealthy dependence. Psychology and personal growth don't show up on his radar of interest. He's loose with finances, believing that money comes and goes, and when it comes it should be enjoyed. He lives for sports, as a spectator and a participant. His passion is tennis, which he adores and plays at least twice a week.

One would think that two people with such conflicting interests and personalities would have a hard time reconciling their differences. Yet practically without exception Flossy and Gabe's friends would say that this couple has one of the most loving relationships they have ever seen. Their secret? They both see the basis of their connection as something that is far greater than personal style, preference, or interest. The foundation of their relationship is respect and love for each other, and a commitment to extend that respect and love into the other relationships in their lives. They occasionally have disagreements, but those disputes rarely damage or diminish the quality of their love for each other because they value their common ground far more than their individual perspectives. And alongside their differences they share important values, commitments, and activities that bring fun and fulfillment into their lives, such as their beloved daughter and their mutual loves of dancing, sex, art, and music. They are committed to supporting whatever will promote each other's well-being and happiness, not only because they love and want the best for each other, but because they know that their partner's happiness will flow into their own life.

Early in marriage, many of us try to make over the other person to become more like ourselves. It takes a while to realize that making room for differences to peacefully coexist is a better use of precious life energy. When we become wiser, with fewer illusions, we can use our energy more strategically. We don't waste as much time trying to "fix" the other person. It's not resignation that allows the differences to simply be; it's an attitude that we cultivate with practice over time. Fulfilled partners don't become homogeneous over the years; they become more uniquely themselves. Not everything can be worked out, nor need it be. We can learn to live with our differences. One of the keys to a successful marriage lies in accepting and respecting the differences — letting them enrich us, rather than trying to eliminate them. While this is easier said than done, cultivating the qualities of acceptance, tolerance, and understanding will serve you and all of your relations for a lifetime.

37

Your opinion is not the truth.

Georgia and Kelly were both firefighters. They were each committed to their physical health and fitness and spent time every day running, stretching, and weight training at the gym. They were each nearly perfect physical specimens. In their first couple's session, Georgia said, "I don't feel safe in our relationship. I'm constantly tense and afraid that he's going to criticize me." Practically before she got the words out, Kelly jumped in. "I can't trust her. She lies. I know when there's something wrong, and it drives me crazy when she won't tell me." They were competing with each other to prove to me that the other was at fault.

This behavior reflected the blaming cycle that the two had been locked in for most of their relationship. I suggested that they consider that it wasn't just their bodies that required regular and frequent workouts, but their emotions as well. After some explanation, they both agreed that the concept made sense, although it was difficult for them to understand what that might mean or look like. Like many young couples, they were operating under the notion that a good relationship just happens when two people love each other. After challenging this notion, I gave them some guidelines for the process of emotional fitness: tell the truth of your experience. In other words, express your feelings, not your opinions and judgments. Risk vulnerability by asking for what you want. Don't withhold. Speak up more, even when you are afraid.

Kelly didn't have much trouble speaking up. His challenge had more to do with developing self-restraint and learning to be a better listener. To do so, he needed to become more patient, ask more questions, and hold back when he felt the impulse to offer his judgments or advice unless Georgia specifically solicited it. They were both so habituated to throwing around their opinions and accusations that they often seemed unaware of doing it. "You're always making us late!" "You don't tell me what time we have to be there!" "You don't listen to me!" "You always interrupt!" "You make me so mad!" "You don't care about me!" "You're just like your mother!" It was a nearly continuous cycle, the result of which was a deep erosion of the love and affection that had previously infused their relationship.

Fortunately Kelly and Georgia were good students. They wanted their marriage to work more than they wanted to be right about their problems being the other person's fault. They took on the challenge with the same level of commitment that they brought to their physical workouts. Within a few months, their relationship transformed. Georgia and Kelly committed themselves to deleting all unsolicited judgments, advice, and opinions. They diligently replaced the critical remarks with statements of feeling, questions, and sincere interest. This simple (but not easy) discipline made them trust each other more than they ever had before.

Many people believe that they are speaking the truth, when, in fact, they are only sharing their thoughts, opinions, criticisms, and judgments. Unlike our opinions, truth is irrefutable and beyond question. Truth invites openness, and it needs no explanation or justification. It also rarely provokes attacking responses. It simply is. As we learn to distinguish truth from opinion and speak accordingly — that is, in a respectful and nonjudgmental way — our relationships with others and our experience of ourselves become richer and more authentic.

38

*Vacations are necessities,
not luxuries.*

CHARLIE: My family never took vacations when I was a kid. Consequently, I grew up thinking getaways were not important and only for other people. Over the years, and with Linda's help, I've found that neither of these notions is true. As an adult I've learned that a vacation doesn't have to take place in a faraway, exotic land, and it doesn't have to cost a lot of money. It can occur anywhere and anytime that we are temporarily relieved of the ordinary responsibilities of daily life. As long as there is the will, there are ways to take time off that don't require you to finance a second mortgage on your home. Even better, when we disengage from the demands of our busy lives, we can reexperience the passion and romance that originally brought us together. A change of scenery can reinvigorate our relationship. We are then more apt to see the beauty in our partner and have the time to feel and express our appreciation for them. Being away from the routine of our lives also offers us a fresh perspective that can open our eyes to new possibilities for the future.

Since it's hard to miss what you never had, I never lobbied for vacations in the early years of our marriage. In fact, I often resisted Linda's efforts to have us take time off together. I'd say, "We can't afford it," or, "There are other things I'd rather spend that kind of money on," or, later, with the kids bickering and fighting, "It'll be the vacation from hell." I'm grateful to Linda for persisting in her efforts. I've since become a true believer in this kind of time off, and these days it's often I who tends to initiate our breaks — the long ones as well as the short ones.

LINDA: A year into parenthood, I was at my wit's end. Our firstborn, Jesse, was an intensely energetic, active, and loud child. I didn't sleep much the entire year. I got to the point where I felt that my sense of self was being sucked out of me along with the breast milk. I knew that I needed a change of scenery, but we had little money because I wasn't working and Charlie was still in graduate school. I spoke to my friend Carole, who lived near the beach on the north shore of Boston. She told me that she was going to the mountains for a week, and she offered to let us stay at her home while she was away.

It was wonderful! Jesse loved the ocean, and being away from home gave us a new slant on life. I still shopped, but in a different market. I still prepared meals, but in a different kitchen. Charlie and I shared some wonderful times there.

Life seemed sweeter because I didn't feel empty, and I started to enjoy nursing again. I learned a huge lesson that summer about how to take care of myself and how to take care of our family. I realized how important it is to get away on a regular basis. Vacations don't have to cost much, and we don't have to go very far from home, but we do need to go. By interrupting our normal pattern, we not only gain a fresh perspective, but we get to rest, refresh, and recharge. No matter how little time or money you think you have, you just can't afford not to take vacations!

39

*Trust takes years to establish
and moments to destroy.*

CHARLIE: Relationships don't begin with trust. Trust must be built day-by-day by two people who demonstrate trustworthiness through their words and actions. Trust is developed conversation by conversation, by working through conflicts and demonstrating kindness, generosity, and consideration. In a moment of unconsciousness, anger, or fear, we can do great damage to the trust that we have worked so diligently to create. Yet breakdowns inevitably occur. We can't avoid them, but we can repair the damage, provided there is a shared intention to do so. The more awake and aware we are of the preciousness of trust, the more deliberate we will be in protecting and preserving it.

Although our legal system says "innocent until proven guilty," when it comes to relationships, most of us don't start with this assumption. It's not that we're all a bunch of paranoids; it's just that most of us don't get to adulthood without having been burned by people who we thought were trustworthy. Emotional betrayal makes us much less naive and more cautious. While we all would like to believe that people are generally trustworthy, most of us have abundant evidence to the contrary.

In the early stages of our relationship, I trusted that Linda was a good person, that she would never do anything to deliberately hurt me, that she was honest and decent, and that she could be counted on to honor her word and keep her commitments. Yet on a more subtle level, there were aspects of Linda that I didn't trust at all. I not only kept these feelings from her, I wasn't even aware of them myself. I didn't trust that she'd stay with me if I failed to be a good provider. I didn't trust her to not say things to me that would hurt my feelings. I didn't trust that she would never take advantage of my vulnerability if I let my guard down and shared my deepest fears and longings. I feared that she would say bad things about me behind my back to our children and turn them against me.

These fears had little to do with Linda and much more to do with patterns that I had taken on from my own childhood. I came into our relationship with my own emotional baggage, as most people do. It took me a while to begin to see that Linda was more trustworthy than many of the other people in my life. Consequently, I frequently tested her caring, not trusting it to be unconditional. Fortunately, Linda hung in there until I came to realize that it wasn't just her that I didn't trust, it was me. I didn't trust myself to provide for my inner needs and concerns because I had turned that responsibility over to others throughout my life. This realization did more to affect the level of trust in our relationship than all of Linda's efforts combined.

As I accepted responsibility for meeting the needs of my own well-being instead of expecting Linda to provide for it, the level of trust in our relationship began to climb. By acting in ways that gave me evidence that I was self-caring, self-respecting, and self-reliant, I experienced an increased sense of trust in myself. I made and kept promises to myself that I had in the past been willing to break; I strove to bring more compassion and kindness to my self-talk, to be less judgmental, and to take better care of my body; and I gave myself more of the kindness, respect, and appreciation that I had been looking to Linda and others to provide. The result was that Linda felt less obliged to take care of me, and without this pressure she was more loving and free when she was around me. It was a net gain for us both, as the quality and quantity of what she gave to me increased. As it did, I reciprocated, and the trust level between us increased dramatically, eventually creating a rock-solid foundation for our relationship.

We still at times can experience momentary feelings of doubt or mistrust, but when we lapse it's always very brief, just a temporary blip on the screen that soon disappears. These days, one of my greatest pleasures, and Linda's too, is to relax into the trust that now characterizes our marriage. It doesn't get any better than this.

40

*Ultimatums and threats
do more harm than good.*

Ultimatums and threats are aggressive manipulations, which stem from fear and generate defensiveness. They are essentially a grab for control. The person who is the target of ultimatums and threats is hard-pressed to stay open to negotiate in good faith. Strong-arm tactics only result in fear-based behavior. Even if the bully gets his or her way, the victory comes with a huge price tag.

Mack and Phyllis sought out marriage counseling because there was so much pain in their relationship. Every few months a horrible scene would occur over issues that included sex, money, house decorating, and car buying — the usual. On those occasions when their angry interchanges escalated to the boiling point, Phyllis would start ranting. "Tomorrow I'm calling the real estate agent to put this house on the market, and I'm calling the divorce lawyer too. I can't take this abuse!" Mack was usually the patient one, reassuring Phyllis that things would improve and reminding her that there was a lot about their marriage that was worth saving. Then things would settle down until the next blowup.

Mack's steadiness soothed Phyllis and calmed her when she became explosive. This pattern lulled them both into a false sense of security. They both believed that his job was to cool Phyllis's volatility, and that Mack always would, since he always had. Consequently, Phyllis never felt the need to learn how to manage her own temper. What neither of them expected was that Mack would quit his job as marital moderator. Their increasingly frequent outbursts were taking more of a toll on their marriage than either of them had realized. One day Phyllis once again threatened to file for divorce if Mack didn't give in to her demands. During this particularly painful outburst, the cycle finally broke. This time Mack didn't try to appease her. "Okay. Just go ahead then; do it," he said. "I can't live this way anymore." Phyllis didn't believe that he meant it, but he did. Within two weeks, they were separated. Mack moved out and got a place of his own.

Phyllis was shocked. She realized this was no manipulation on his part. He meant it. She'd thought that she would be able to go on indefinitely indulging in her manipulative tactics. But everyone has his limit, and Mack had reached his. He had lost the will to keep going, even to keep trying. In the next few counseling sessions, Phyllis was deeply remorseful over how dishonest she had been. She admitted that she loved Mack, that she wanted very badly for the marriage to continue, and that she even loved the house that she had kept threatening to sell. She acknowledged that all of her threats were empty and that she finally realized what she really wanted. But it was too late — Mack wasn't willing to go back to her. It was a painful lesson for Phyllis, but it helped her become more responsible in how she expressed herself, a lesson that she never forgot.

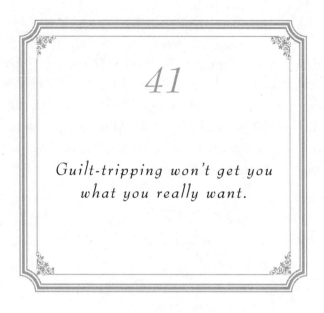

41

Guilt-tripping won't get you what you really want.

LINDA: I come from a long line of guilt-trippers. My ancestors adopted the bizarre idea that if you made a person feel guilty, he wouldn't repeat an undesirable behavior. Honoring the family tradition, I used this tactic in my marriage for years. I noticed, however, that despite my best efforts, unwanted behaviors continued. Charlie and I both always ended up feeling bad. Faultfinding left me with a sour taste in my mouth and a feeling of loneliness.

What does one do about a destructive pattern that has been in the family for generations? I decided to risk disloyalty to the family tradition and vowed to resist the temptation to manipulate by guilt. Instead, I practiced keeping my attention on myself rather than focusing on what I didn't like about Charlie. I replaced "You never spend any time with me" with "I love being with you. When are you available for us to have some fun this week?" Instead of "We never go anywhere new and interesting," I tried "How about going to the beach for the weekend? I'll make the reservations and arrange for child care." Although I don't always get what I want, more often than not I do. More important, those residual negative feelings that once left me feeling resentful and miserable are a thing of the past.

42

Give what you want to receive.

Lucille was six feet tall, big-boned, strong, and a few years older than her husband, Dennis. He was slight of build, gentle, and sensitive. Lucille was outspoken and direct. She projected an air of confidence in social situations, but her inner feelings reflected a different reality. She often felt insecure and unlovable, and she used her imposing physical presence to cover up self-doubt. Lucille also continually tried to extract reassurance about her sex appeal and attractiveness from Dennis. Although he tried to demonstrate his love for her, his efforts were often half-hearted, and Lucille continued to feel anxious and unsatisfied.

One day a friend of Lucille's died suddenly of a brain aneurysm. As she mourned, Lucille experienced her own vulnerability — the part of herself that had been hiding behind an image of great strength and competence. Lucille started speaking more openly about the truth of her fear, loneliness, and confusion, and about how much she loved Dennis, and he then found it easy to respond to her. Her open heart opened his, in a way that her coercion never could. And his attention was infinitely more gratifying because it was freely given.

Out of her gratitude for Dennis's genuine caring, Lucille found herself giving him the kind of acknowledgment that she desired for herself. He responded in kind. Most of us have discovered the hard way that trying to get someone to give you what you want doesn't often bring about the desired outcome. Why then is it that so many of us continue to use control and manipulation, both direct and covert, to try to coerce our partner into delivering the goods? For one thing, there aren't a lot of obvious alternatives.

Giving what you value rather than trying to get it is an approach that can produce very positive results, provided that you possess at least a minimal amount of trust and patience. For example, instead of trying to get your partner to understand you, try a little harder to understand them, not only what they're saying but also how they're feeling. Instead of competing to be heard, let them have their say, listen intently, don't interrupt, and don't respond until you've checked with them to make sure that they've finished talking. Instead of trying to get them to express affection to you, show them your caring and appreciation in the most creative and sincere ways that you can. It's easier for us to give more to others when we feel deeply attended to; in general, the impulse to reciprocate arises spontaneously in them. The feeling of gratitude ignites our desire to give, and these gifts are infinitely more satisfying than those given in response to coercion or manipulation.

43

Don't neglect your friends
just because you've
acquired a spouse.

Nancy and Leslie had been best friends for years. They went on vacations together and shared everything. When Nancy fell in love, Leslie was happy that her dear friend had finally found a good man. As the courtship unfolded, however, they spent progressively less time together. When Leslie called, she got Nancy's voice mail most of the time, and their enjoyable outings became fewer and further between.

Leslie missed Nancy terribly, and finally, after Nancy and her boyfriend had married, there was a face-to-face confrontation. Leslie told Nancy how neglected and rejected she felt. Nancy was defensive, saying she was terribly busy trying to keep her nursing career afloat, with the remainder of her time absorbed by this man who was literally "the answer to my prayers." Leslie stood her ground. "It's because I care so much about you and our friendship that I have to tell you this. You've dropped all your friends. Look at your life over the last year. Between falling in love, planning the wedding, and then the honeymoon, no one has even seen you except on your wedding day."

Nancy spent the next few days thinking about what Leslie had said. Most of her friends had, in fact, drifted away. Leslie was the only one who cared enough to fight for their relationship. She thanked Leslie for her honesty and vowed to start taking better care of their friendship. Less than two weeks later, Nancy was thrown by a horse, sustaining a severe break in her leg. In the ensuing months of healing, she needed the closeness of her friend. Four months after Nancy broke her leg, Leslie became a single mom. Although Nancy's new husband was attentive to her during her recovery, she was immobilized and alone all day while he was at work. Leslie's life, too, was dramatically changed after her son arrived. Leslie's visits assisted Nancy to feel less isolated, and Nancy played an important role as honorary auntie of Leslie's son. These two now needed each other more than ever, and they were both deeply grateful for the restoration of their friendship.

In the throes of newfound love, it can seem inconceivable that any relationship in our life can come close to matching the ecstatic bliss that we find with our new partner. Many of us make the mistake of neglecting our old friends when we are immersed in our new romance. Even our most loyal friends will lose patience with us if we become unavailable to them for long enough. We all have a variety of interpersonal needs, many of which cannot be filled by our primary partner. Regardless of how great things are in our relationship, if we lose our other friendships, our life will be diminished, and so will the amount of richness that we bring to our marriage.

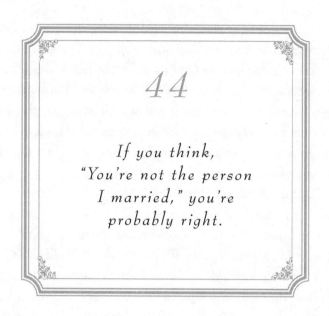

44

*If you think,
"You're not the person
I married," you're
probably right.*

LINDA: My friend Sophie told me that she looked over at her husband Ray one day, with his "skinny little legs" sticking out of his bathrobe, and thought, "I should have done better than this." This was a challenging moment for her because she realized that she didn't get "the prize" after all. Ray was still the tall, thin guy she married, only now his hair was a lot thinner and gray, and he was sixty years old. He hadn't exercised much over the years, and she assessed him as not having aged very gracefully. In the meantime, Sophie's career had taken off, and she was spending her workdays with dynamic, creative, and accomplished women and men. Her professional success had given her an inflated idea of herself. Looking at Ray now, he seemed aged and shabby, like an old, worn-out shoe. Indeed, Ray had changed. In their early years, he had struggled valiantly to compete and achieve in his career. He had done well, but he was no longer driven by the hunger for power and success that had possessed him for much of his adult life; it was time to wind down and enjoy life more. Now he immersed himself in the simple pleasures of home and family. He baked bread and muffins to share with Sophie. He loved working in their garden, cutting and arranging fresh flowers as a meditative practice.

Sophie, on the other hand, felt liberated when their children left home, and she dove headlong into her career. With time and deep reflection, Sophie realized that her choice was difficult for Ray at this point in the cycle of his life. He had been looking forward to slowing down so he could enjoy time together with his wife, and she was committed to working and flying around the globe. Sophie realized in her reflection that in some ways she wasn't such a prize either. In so doing, she was able to appreciate Ray more, without putting herself down. She saw that they were, both literally and figuratively, deserving of each other. Neither of them was superior or inferior to the other, simply distinct in their own uniqueness.

Sophie decided to stay in the marriage with Ray, skinny legs and all, and went on to cocreate a deep, loving connection with him, one that could include the flaws and imperfections they both possessed, as well as their great gifts.

When we marry, we are full of illusion and expectation. Generally, we haven't been together for enough years to know each other fully. As our partners grow and change and reveal themselves, we are challenged to adapt and accept them for who they are. To the degree that we can do this, we are likely to experience the same from them. This does not mean, of course, tolerating behaviors that are disrespectful or abusive, but accepting aspects of their personality that are not in keeping with our concept of the ideal mate. Change is the only constant in life. Marriage provides a great curriculum for learning to accept the inevitability of change in each other, ourselves, and the world.

45

Resisting the temptation to prove your point will win you a lot of points.

CHARLIE: For years, I always had to rub it in when I was right. I was driven by my desire to impress Linda and others with my intelligence, and by the adrenaline rush of decisively driving my point home in an argument. It was so important to me that I would frequently lose sight of the consequences of my indulgence. I would press loudly onward until I was either proven wrong (in my eyes, this happened rarely, as I was usually closed to conflicting opinion) or I got the final say. The thrill of this victory would be followed by a kind of defeat, as trust, closeness, and caring were inevitably sacrificed. I'm a slow learner, so it took me a long time to realize that these losses far outweighed the momentary pleasures of my victory. I was winning the arguments, but losing the real prize.

These days, I'm rarely tempted to drive my point home — the need to be right just isn't as compelling as it used to be, as I've stopped feeding that desire the way I used to. Bad habits weaken and eventually die when we stop indulging them. The result for me has been a strengthening of the quality of goodwill and sweetness in my marriage, which has made it all the more worthwhile.

At first, however, even after I found the motivation to break the self-righteousness habit, letting go of being right proved to be more of a challenge than I'd expected. I found that when I didn't try to prove my point, I often felt susceptible to feeling blamed and wrong myself. Preemptively blaming others had enabled me to feel less vulnerable to the possibility of others' criticisms and attacks. Now I felt naked and unprotected without the defense of my intellectually combative strategies. Ultimately, I learned that the best defense is the truth of my experience, which unlike defensiveness does not invite attack or aggression.

Learning to recognize the ways in which I have emotionally armed myself and finding the courage and strength to disarm has been one of the hardest challenges of my life. It has also been one of the most rewarding. In giving up my need to prove my point, I discovered a degree of trust, openness, and connection with Linda and others that I had never even imagined. Being relieved of this burden has left me feeling freer, lighter, and more relaxed than ever before. And contrary to my fears, the world seems to have become a safer rather than a more dangerous place. Go figure.

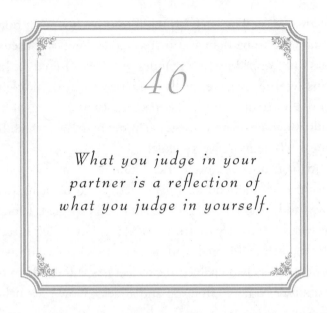

46

What you judge in your partner is a reflection of what you judge in yourself.

LINDA: When we were college students, it used to drive me nuts that Charlie was so laid back. He didn't knock himself out studying and still did well in school. Later, when we were both working, he always found time to play and relax. I judged him as lacking in ambition and drive. The truth is I thought he was lazy. There was an uneasy undercurrent in our relationship that left me feeling rankled whenever he would take time off. Over the years, I came to realize that I was intensely envious because he took such good care of himself.

Eventually, as I came to terms with these feelings, instead of judging him I became able to learn from him. I began to use our relationship as a mirror to find out what I was rejecting and denying in myself. This was quite a demanding practice, but it ultimately proved to be very rewarding. I discovered that I was especially afraid that if I accepted my "inner slug," I would get nothing done and turn into a slob, or, worse still, that people would see me as the lazy good-for-nothing I inwardly feared I might be! Through this process I gradually became more tolerant of what I deemed to be my flaws. Over time, I learned to see them not as flaws at all, but simply as inclinations, desires, feelings, and traits. They were neither inherently negative nor positive aspects of myself. This process helped me to become more accepting of myself and less judgmental of others. As I identified my disowned parts, I made a place for them in my life.

It is an enormous gift to our partner when we do our own work. As we grow more tolerant of all aspects of ourselves, we are easier to be with, for our partner and within ourselves. In the growing acceptance of self, we become less judgmental of others. Our experience of acceptance and nonjudgment is like a magnet that draws others into our lives. It's strange how these wonderful qualities are generated out of judgments that were once the source of so much pain. But then, isn't it often the case that our greatest gifts arise from our most difficult experiences?

47

Your partner is your teacher and your student.

A primary law of relationships is that we are not attracted to someone who is just like us. The phenomenon of complementarity dictates that in general we will be attracted to people who are very different from, or perhaps in some ways even the opposite of, ourselves. The reason for this is simple. Within each of us there is an intrinsic longing to experience wholeness. This yearning draws us to people who are more developed in certain areas than we are. Unfortunately, the same qualities that attract us initially to our partner can start driving us crazy after the infatuation wears off. The very lessons that we unconsciously invited this person into our life to teach us, we will resist. Rather than appreciate the opportunities that our partner's differences provide for us to learn, grow, and expand our sense of self, we are more apt to resent

120

their differences, feel threatened and annoyed by them, and try to get them to change — that is, to become more like they should be . . . that is, more like us! In the meantime, they are, of course, doing the same thing. Is it any wonder that so many couples get into power struggles?

Tony was a conscientious, reliable, and responsible man. He was always the designated driver when he and his partner, Abel, went out with friends. Abel was a musician. In his work at the recording studio, he was in constant collaboration with creative, artistic people. Tony kept the home fires burning while Abel worked late nights and weekends. Tony resented the unpredictable nature of Abel's schedule, and the wild swings in Abel's income rattled him.

Abel chafed at Tony's efforts to get him to change. Tony wanted him to lead a more stable life, to drink less, and to rein in his volatile temper. Abel thought that Tony was trying to domesticate him and squelch his creative passion. They were in a constant struggle for power and control that nearly ruined their relationship. Finally, they each came to recognize the consequences of their battles and the fears that underlay their efforts to control each other. They came to appreciate that they each had gifts for the other, and that although these gifts were not always easy to accept, they held the possibility of deeply enriching the quality of their individual lives and their relationship.

Gradually Abel became more able (pun intended) to be open to Tony's influence, and he introduced more discipline and focus into his life. He came to value a more restrained approach to relating his dissatisfaction, and rather than blowing up at Tony when he was upset, he expressed his grievances in more responsible and respectful ways. He stopped the chronic outbursts at work that had caused a parade of disgruntled employees to quit. With stable and consistent help, Abel's business became more profitable. He was astonished to find that he could manage his emotions without stifling his creative expression.

Tony, on the other hand, learned from Abel to permit himself to take risks and become more adventurous. He quit his high-paying job to follow a dream he had denied himself for several years. He enrolled in college as a full-time student. He loved being back in school, and he got straight As. He had learned from Abel to give himself over to his heart's desire and to trust that things would somehow work out.

Whether we consciously know it or not, we have much to learn from, as well as much to teach, our partner. However, some of us are more comfortable in the role of the knowing teacher, others in the role of the receptive student. Those who are comfortable as the student freely and easily open to learn from their partner. But these people may be uncomfortable with the responsibility of being the knowing, accomplished, and capable one. For those who are more comfortable in the role of the teacher, their stretch is to own their humility. Sometimes, we need to grow into one role or the other. Ideally in a relationship both partners develop the flexibility to shift from one role to the other, and the wisdom to know when these shifts are necessary. In time, the dance can become so seamless, so effortless, that the distinctions of teacher and student disappear and there are just the two lovers learning from and serving each other. We come to understand that there is a deep, intuitive knowing that brings couples together in the first place. The best relationships are those in which both partners become adept in both roles, each at turns embodying the wisdom and strength of the teacher and the openness and humility of the student.

48

*Commitment is not
a one-time event;
it's an ongoing process.*

LINDA: I once met a creative, dynamic man named Ken. When he got married, he enjoyed his wedding day so much that he said to his wife, "We should do this every year!" And they have, seventeen times. They have gotten married in many different traditions: by a Baptist minister in the French West Indies; in an Anglican ceremony in England; by the skiing judge in Vail, Colorado; by a kahuna on the beach in Hawaii. Once they got married on shipboard by an Episcopalian minister sailor; they had a Buddhist ceremony at the San Francisco Zen Center; and one year, Al Huang, a tai chi master, married them in a ceremony at the Esalen Institute in Big Sur, California. A Mexican judge once married them in Cabo San Lucas with a mariachi band playing, and the next year they got married near Tucson by a Navaho elder who brought his family in native garb to bear witness to the ceremony.

Ken and his wife, Maddy, alternate years coordinating the event. The ministers always get a big thrill out of marrying a couple that has a strong history of commitment, rather than wondering, as they often do, "How long will this marriage last?"

Each year, there are new vows, a new officiator, a new photographer, and, of course, always a honeymoon. The pictures in the photo album of each ceremony show the changes in their lives. There are shots of Maddy with a big belly from each of her two pregnancies. And, of course, their aging shows in their faces. When they look at the pictures, they remember some of the hardships they have gone through together. Ken told me that every time he participates in a ceremony, he comes away profoundly moved, with some new understanding about himself and the relationship. The cost — about two hundred dollars for the officiator, plus an additional cost for the photographer — seems a small price to pay for the tremendous value they derive from the renewal of their vows and the ritual of once again declaring their love and commitment to each other.

It's been obvious to me for a long time that we don't just commit to a relationship once. We commit countless times. We commit when we become engaged, at the legal marriage ceremony, and each time we have a child together. But there is also a series of often unnoticed recommitments that are profoundly important. These are the ones that follow periods of doubt, disappointment, and stress, the dark periods in the marriage that, at times, can threaten its very viability. When we manage to navigate the darkness and come through to a period of renewal and light, there is cause for great celebration and rejoicing.

For years, Charlie and I have been renewing our vows and writing new ones. Sometimes we exchange vows on our wedding anniversary, sometimes on Valentine's Day, sometimes on New Year's Day. Each year we make sure to go away for a honeymoon. What is important is not so much what we do or where we go, but that we intentionally reinfuse our connection with a renewed commitment to love and support each other, at ever-deepening levels. These affirmations enrich our relationship profoundly, strengthen the bond between us, and continually remind us of the refuge and love we envisioned on our wedding day.

49

*Generosity of spirit
is the foundation of
great relationships.*

Ursala grew up in Germany during the Second World War.
She had vivid memories of the terror of the bombings, the
food shortages, and the children orphaned by the ravages of
war. When she married Pete, both of their former spouses
had died and their children were grown. When Ursala was
sixty and Pete was seventy-five, she saw a film at her church
about a group of orphans living in Russia. Her heart went
out to a crippled four-year-old boy who could only scoot
around with the use of his hands and arms and was considered unadoptable. She couldn't get this child out of her
mind. She talked with Pete about adopting the boy.
Although Pete had loved raising his own children, at seventy-
five he was shocked at the thought of starting over with a
new family. But he saw how important this was to Ursala.

Pete struggled with the part of himself that wanted to rest in his easy chair in his retirement and the part that wanted his wife to have all the things that were important to her. Out of his love and devotion to his wife, Pete made the extraordinary choice to agree to adopt the boy. It was an act of supreme generosity, both to the young boy and to his wife. The negotiations for a foreign adoption were demanding, but Ursala persisted and obtained the go-ahead to fly to Russia to bring Alosha home.

Pete and Ursala fell in love with this adorable, intelligent, spirited child. He learned English in a matter of weeks, soon refusing to speak Russian. He seemed to be putting his difficult life in the Russian orphanage behind him. With extensive medical assessments, doctors determined that his legs would have to be amputated below the knees. He was fitted with prostheses and, thanks to his spirit and determination, was soon walking on them.

Alosha has become the central focus of this couple's life. Ursala and Pete report being closer than ever. There was generosity on both their parts to welcome a disabled boy from a different culture into their lives. They learned that if Alosha had grown up in the orphanage, because of the terrible overcrowding he would have been put out to fend for himself at age fourteen. They are grateful to have such a bright light in their family and swear that this boy keeps them young. Their own generosity of spirit has enlivened this couple's life.

50

*If your partner is being
defensive, you may be giving
them reason to be.*

CHARLIE: "You're being defensive!" I yelled at Linda, and of course I was right. It didn't matter to me that I had played a big part in her feeling the need to be defensive. When someone is attacked and feels that they are in hostile territory, the urge to defend inevitably arises.

A little knowledge is truly a dangerous thing. In the earlier days of our relationship, a *little* knowledge is all I had. I had enough knowledge to recognize Linda's defensiveness, but not enough to recognize my part in it. I had enough knowledge to engage, often successfully, in power games, but not enough to see the consequences of my competitiveness. I had enough knowledge to maintain the upper hand, but not enough to manage to put down my weapons when they were causing more harm than good. I accused Linda of being defensive more times than I care to admit, trying to get the focus of attention off of me and onto her.

Although I can be a slow learner, I generally remember the lessons that are the hardest to learn. This one was particularly tough for me, but I finally got it in the depth of my bones: "The better you listen, the less defensive your partner will be." Instead of trying to get your partner to become less defensive, ask yourself, "What might I be doing that could be contributing to her feeling unsafe?" The moment of consciousness that gives rise to the question breaks the cycle of escalating tension. You can ask yourself the question and you can also ask the other person: "Is there something that I am doing that is causing you to feel unsafe or uncomfortable?" It's the genuine curiosity and concern for your partner that opens a deeper connection and breaks the impasse of mistrust.

Instead of trying to get our partner to lay down their sword and shield first, the challenge is to be courageous enough to do it ourselves. If we do that, they are invited into vulnerability rather than pushed into it. This process of personal disarmament, of disengaging ourselves of our protective mechanisms in the face of danger, requires great courage and commitment. Yet this is precisely what a committed partnership calls forth from us if we are to honor each other and ourselves in a loving way. It's difficult at first, but with practice we can cultivate a taste for the rawness, and over time we can come to enjoy the vast energy that our openness activates within ourselves and in the relationship itself.

51

Marriage isn't 50/50;
it's 100/100.

Simon and Celeste hadn't been married very long when Celeste began to feel uncomfortable in the relationship. Although Simon made a great deal more money than Celeste, they had agreed to split all of their expenses straight down the middle. When it was time to pay the rent, they put in identical amounts. This was the policy for all their expenses: gas and electricity, water, groceries, even newspaper delivery. When they cleaned their apartment, they did it together. Simon felt a sense of pride in the "fairness" of their arrangement. When he massaged Celeste, he kept track of the time, making a note of it and posting it on the refrigerator until he received an equivalent massage from her.

At the occasional times when Celeste mildly protested about the notes on the refrigerator door, Simon dismissed her concerns as being petty. Celeste did not respect her own inner promptings, which were telling her she was selling herself out. She didn't like the policy, but she was afraid to take a stand. Rather than risk confronting Simon, she chose to swallow her feelings and stay quiet about her dissatisfaction. It didn't work, and Celeste found herself sinking into a mood of gloom. During this time, her mother decided to fly in from the East Coast for a weeklong stay. Celeste got a momentary lift anticipating the visit. She and Simon cleaned the apartment until it sparkled, neither of them knowing that their life was about to take a huge turn.

At first, Celeste's mom didn't say much. She silently observed her daughter and son-in-law interacting and read the charts and notes on the refrigerator. After a few days, Celeste's mother couldn't remain silent any longer. "I don't like what I'm seeing here. Simon conducts this marriage like a business deal. Marriage isn't a business. Is this what you really want?"

Celeste was shocked by her mother's words and burst into tears. She told her how miserable she had become over the months, how dry and brittle she was feeling, and how unhappy she felt over her failed attempts to reach Simon. Celeste's mother left with a pledge from her daughter that she would inform Simon of what she was feeling and that despite her discomfort she would be strong and direct in speaking with him.

Simon listened to her complaints and responded that he liked their arrangement just fine, that it was fair and equitable, and that it worked for him. Celeste insisted that it wasn't working for her and that if they couldn't settle this issue on their own they would have to get help from a third party. Simon refused to go to marriage counseling. "They just want to take your money and you end up having to fix your marriage yourself. Besides, most marriage counselors are women, and they can't help but take the woman's side against the man. You can't expect them to be unbiased. It's a waste of money."

Celeste had silently gone along with the old policy for so many months that she had led Simon to believe that she was satisfied, when in fact she wasn't. Meanwhile, Simon's ostensible concern about equity concealed a deep level of mistrust in the marriage. Although he claimed that his stance was about fairness and equality, it was essentially an outgrowth of a worldview in which he perceived women as untrustworthy and inclined to taking advantage of their partners financially and materially. Consequently, when Celeste urged Simon to reconsider his position, he was unwilling to compromise on their agreement. In seeing how rigidly attached Simon was to his self-protection and seeing that there was nothing that she could do to win his trust, Celeste let go of the marriage and moved out. Not surprisingly, Simon made no effort to reconcile their differences or reunite after the separation.

"I knew practically from the beginning that something was wrong between us," Celeste admitted after the divorce. "I just hoped that if I kept trying, Simon would eventually trust me and come around. I guess I should have been more honest from the beginning about how frustrated I was feeling. Next time I will be."

52

*Trust can be rebuilt,
even after a painful betrayal,
but it may require hard work.*

When Kristie and Forrest got married, Kristie was so naive that she actually believed the trust she felt at the time of the ceremony would remain constant, or if it changed it would only become stronger. So it came as quite a shock to her to discover that trust level goes both up and down in every relationship. When they hit their first painful trust-busting crisis — Forrest's one-night stand — Kristie wanted so badly to live in the fantasy that everything was just peachy that at first she couldn't even acknowledge the loss. Once she faced the truth, Kristie fell into despair, fearing that their radiant relationship was besmirched by a hideous black mark that could never be erased. She saw this awful disappointment as the beginning of the end of their relationship, and she concluded that they could never recover from it.

These two had a lot to learn about restoring trust. The first thing Kristie had to do was to confront Forrest with her feelings of hurt and disappointment. Then she had to meet the challenge of taking him down off the pedestal and accepting his flaws and inadequacies. On the other hand, she had to resist the temptation to play holier-than-thou, with herself as the righteous one and Forrest as the lowly sinner. From this difficult breakdown, they both acquired a more mature perspective, recognizing that they each have foibles and blind spots, as well as competencies and strengths.

They spent the next several months having numerous discussions about the conditions of their marriage that gave rise to the infidelity. Kristie had to speak from a compassionate perspective without blame or defensiveness in order to create an atmosphere of safety. It took a long time for her to accomplish this. By taking responsibility for her part in the breakdown, she created a safe space for Forrest to speak with vulnerability about his part in the broken trust. He was open with her about how he had felt smothered by her possessiveness and had acted out rather than speaking to her directly. He had been immature that night, drinking too much and acting like a single guy.

They both learned the lessons embedded in their mistakes, about forgiveness and making amends. Early on, neither Kristie nor Forrest had any idea that the marriage could be even stronger and more wonderful than before — not despite the break in trust, but because of it. They both learned that a relationship can take some heavy hits and not only make a full recovery, but become more resilient. The levels of trust can improve because of the learning and attention that is required for repair.

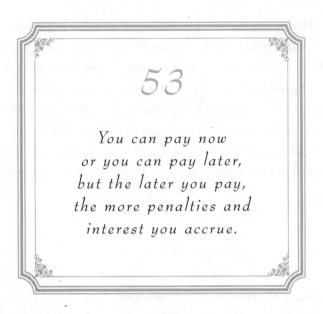

53

*You can pay now
or you can pay later,
but the later you pay,
the more penalties and
interest you accrue.*

Marcy's fortieth birthday was coming up, and she wanted a big party. She asked her husband, Brad, months in advance if he would plan a celebration for her. He knew that he would be in final exams around her birthday but didn't mention it. He just agreed to make the arrangements. As the big day approached, Marcy noticed that not much seemed to be happening. There were no evident arrangements for guests, flowers, music, decorations, food, a cake, or anything. When she finally questioned Brad, he admitted that he hadn't done anything, and that the birthday party was not high on his priority list. Although he had made an agreement with her, he hadn't followed through.

Marcy was terribly disappointed and angry, but she put

her feelings aside to get busy creating the party. The two of them were able to scramble at the last minute and, with the help of friends, put together a terrific birthday party. Marcy's bitterness had been building up, so for several weeks after the party she was withdrawn, cold, and aloof. She was locked into resentment; Brad was paying interest and penalties. He was afraid to bring the subject up, but it was even worse to live in cold silence. He told Marcy that he was truly sorry, that by not being honest from the very beginning he had obviously made a big mess. Brad was vulnerable with Marcy, but she couldn't forgive him right away; for weeks she had been building a case in her mind about how unreliable he was. For her, this was more than a small issue; she was questioning Brad's character.

"If you had just been honest with me about your exams, I could have understood that. I would have called my two sisters and women friends to create the party. You would have only had to play a small part. But because you withheld your true feelings, I proceeded as if I could count on you. That's what really upset me. Now I don't know whether or not you are the kind of person who can be counted on!"

Brad didn't argue. He just listened to her hurt, disappointment, and anger. He knew she had a right to feel the way she did. Instead of trying to prove her wrong, he went about trying to demonstrate that he was in fact trustworthy. Brad understood that Marcy couldn't help questioning whether he was being honest with her, so he began saying "No" when he felt no, rather than trying to bluff when she asked for something. In the next months, he was very deliberate about keeping his agreements and promises. It took some weeks for the diminished trust in their relationship to be repaired. They had both learned how important it is to put the truth out there quickly to avoid the consequences that inevitably result from concealment. Trust was not only restored but was deepened beyond what it had been before.

54

The cheap thrill you get from putting down your partner isn't so cheap.

Faye and Chip had been locked in a struggle for power that was taking an enormous toll on their marriage. Because they both were run by the fear of being dominated and controlled by the other, even the smallest issue could become a huge dispute. They were always jockeying to get the upper hand. Faye would indulge herself by letting judgments fly out of her mouth: "I can't believe you said that! Didn't your parents ever teach you any manners? You are so rude. You never consider anyone else's feelings. You're the most insensitive person I've ever seen. Some people never learn." And Chip was no better. He would give it right back to her: "When are you going to get it right? You never listen! You always interrupt me! You misinterpret everything I say. You're just like your overly sensitive mother. I can't imagine whatever possessed me to marry you!"

If you have ever found yourself saying anything along the lines of the above, then you have been guilty of putting your partner down. Put-downs often provide a rush of pleasure that comes from a brief feeling of superiority and the sense of temporary safety that comes from attacking someone. Pleasurable as this may be, it comes at a high price. In this case, while Chip and Faye were indulging themselves by taking verbal shots at each other, the love with which they had begun their relationship was rapidly eroding. Their efforts to gain the upper hand were damaging their marriage.

By the time they arrived in the marriage counselor's office, they had suffered a great deal from the effects of the cheap shots they had been taking at each other. Each of them was exhausted from the roller coaster ride of being hurt and angry and then patching things up, knowing full well that it was an uneasy truce, that there would only be a brief interlude before the next flare-up. Neither Faye nor Chip could fully relax in their own home. The level of suffering that they were both experiencing provided the motivation to lower their defenses long enough to finally get the help that they had needed for a long time.

In their marriage counseling, they were introduced to the notion of "win-win." This is not so much a strategy of success, but an understanding of the essential reality that in any partnership there is no such thing as win-lose; if what you gain is at your partner's expense, then you both have lost. Like two people riding a tandem bicycle, if one goes down, you both fall. Either you win together or you lose together.

As Faye and Chip gradually became able to understand this, they began working more cooperatively and less adversarially.

When they tried to enact the practice at home, they soon found out that although it is a simple concept, it is not easy to implement change. But because they both wanted desperately to preserve their marriage, they were determined in their attempts to "fight fair." They became more aware of the triggers for accusation and blame and often succeeded in repairing the damage before it was too late. They understood that the put-downs stemmed from relationship patterns that had existed in their families for generations, and that the work that they were doing was not simply for themselves but for their children and grandchildren as well. They knew it was up to them to break the cycles that had resulted in so much pain over the years in each of their original families. Their vision of liberating their children from these painful cycles provided the incentive to commit to doing the work that would ultimately bring them more inner and interpersonal peace. Chip knew that it wasn't an exaggeration when he referred to the effort it took to break his reactive patterns as "Herculean."

Faye and Chip did learn to fight fairly. They learned to disengage from the habituated tendency to indulge in taking cheap shots. They both realized that they could exercise self-restraint, vulnerability, and emotional honesty to create an atmosphere of respect. As they got used to the experience of increased trust and safety, they became less tolerant of behaviors that had formerly been commonplace in their relationship. Verbally abusive patterns all but disappeared, and they achieved a degree of trust and respect that neither of them had imagined possible. "If we can do it," Faye said during our last meeting, "anyone can!"

55

Marriage does require sacrifice, but what you stand to gain is infinitely greater than what you give up.

CHARLIE: Back when I was "commitment-phobic," I was sure that the costs of marriage would outweigh its rewards. Somehow this fear didn't stop me from getting married, but for a while it did stop me from giving myself fully to the relationship. I kept myself partly braced against it and usually put my own needs (or what I thought were my needs) before Linda's. On some half-conscious level I imagined that in this way I would partly compensate for losing my freedom. Not surprisingly, this strategy didn't work. My struggle to maintain control resulted only in increased suffering for both of us. In time I came to realize that the gifts I received were far greater than the preferences that I had given up. Ultimately, Linda's well-being became as important to me as my own. In the process, I experienced greater fulfillment and joy than I had ever known. It turned out that sacrificing my desire for control and gratification in favor of a commitment to intimacy, mutual support, and spiritual growth was what made my cup run over. The outcome would have been a bargain at a hundred times the price!

None of this is to downplay the sacrifices we are sometimes called upon to make in marriage. No, we can't *always* do what we want when we want. At the least, we have to negotiate and coordinate with another person's preferences, tastes, timetable, and styles. We can't always choose the video, the ice cream, the carpet, the restaurant, or the vacation destination. We may at some point be asked to move across the country for a spouse's career, to have fewer or more children than we'd like, or care for aging in-laws. We may even be called upon to go through unforeseen periods of hardship, addiction, depression, serious illness, or tragedy. If we stay together, at some point we will either endure the death of our partner, or our partner will endure ours.

In learning to let go of the need to always have things our way, it becomes possible to create a harmonious relationship that brings a much deeper level of fulfillment than does the gratification of ego-based desire. When we create a shared history with another person, security and trust develop, allowing for a depth of intimacy that's not possible in more superficial relationships. Most important, in all of this we become more loving human beings.

56

Good sex doesn't necessarily make a marriage great, but it sure helps.

Just as good sex can enormously enhance a relationship, sexual dissatisfaction can greatly diminish the quality of connection that a couple shares. It's not simply the sexual act itself that matters, it's the way in which each person views this experience and their willingness to respect the perspective and desires of their partner. Ian and Meredith came into counseling because they had different ideas regarding the frequency of their sexual activity. Ian had a stronger libido, believing that increasing the frequency of their sexual experiences was all that was needed to improve things, while Meredith thought that sex just wasn't so important. They became so polarized that they began to sleep in separate bedrooms.

Meredith rarely enjoyed sex. She was haunted by unhappy memories of being inappropriately touched by her father, and she was reluctant to talk about these traumatic events. When Ian pressured her for sex she would get highly anxious, which just made things worse. In couples' counseling, Ian was encouraged to practice patience and to stop insisting on sex. Meredith began to open up to her long-denied feelings related to her sexual trauma. She worked with a women's group to speak more openly about the incestuous episodes, and in time she was able to banish much of the shame she had carried for years.

After several months of practicing new and nonsexual forms of touch, Ian and Meredith were able to have intercourse. Their sexual healing required considerable effort, but it was fruitful. They came to see their sexuality as an essential aspect of an intimate connection, a means through which love, play, and passion commingle.

The effort that we take to enliven the sexual aspect of our relationship is itself a way of expressing love and nurturing the partnership. At other times we need to bring more patience and restraint into the sexual relationship so that our partner doesn't feel controlled or pressured. Sometimes we need to be more willing to engage sexually, to lean into the other person's world, not as an act of submission or accommodation, but more as a way of bringing pleasure and joy into their life. In the process of doing one's part to bring more juice into the sexual connection, both partners feel more loved and appreciated. By identifying and doing what we can to break the sexual impasse, we not only bring more pleasure into our marriage, we create a heightened sense of gratitude, love, and appreciation.

57

Forgiveness isn't a one-time event; it's a process.

LINDA: Some people are good at letting go, but they may need to learn more about commitment and hanging in there when things get difficult. Others are strong in the commitment department, but they may find it hard to release the tight grip of control, even when that's what the situation calls for. I've always been strong in the area of hanging on, so letting go has been my challenge. In the early years of our marriage, when I felt hurt it was not uncommon for me to spend days, weeks, or months brooding over my wounds and (not so) secretly harboring grudges against Charlie for being hurtful, neglectful, or insensitive toward me. He, on the other hand, generally seemed to be able to disengage from feelings of resentment and hurt very quickly. He would get angry and get over it.

When I felt hurt, there was always a part of me that stubbornly refused to forgive. I didn't want to let go of the anger. It gave me a sense of self-righteous superiority. Over time, however, I began to notice that this was taking its toll on me. When Charlie was working too much and frequently away from home, I was filled with resentment, and the weight of it just ground me down. Even after I committed myself to being more forgiving, I still found it hard to break the habit of grudge holding.

The impulse toward retaliation and punitiveness is strong in many of us, and it gets activated when we feel wronged or betrayed. At times it can seem nearly impossible in the face of these feelings to let down our guard, risk losing the "protection" our grudges provide, and expose ourselves to the risk of further wounds. What ultimately motivated me to break the habit of holding onto resentment was the realization of how much suffering I was causing myself. I was making myself miserable!

In the process, I saw that I was the one in the greatest need of my own forgiveness. I needed to forgive myself for past sins I felt I had committed (such as being an "imperfect" mother and wife) and flaws that I believed characterized my personality and made me unworthy of my own loving acceptance (such as sometimes being irritable and impatient with my family). I also had to forgive myself for being so unforgiving. I had to accept that this habit of holding grudges against myself and others was a learned, not chosen, pattern that was not my fault. I did recognize, however, that at this point in my life I had the power to change this deeply embedded tendency.

I came to understand that this change would take effort, practice, support, time, and lots of patience — and of course there were times when I needed to forgive myself for taking so long to do it. Like the healing of physical wounds, the process of forgiveness takes time and occurs in layers. I needed to see that the very same wounds would continue to happen unless I was truly willing to let go completely and open my heart. It was a delicate balance between not procrastinating and not rushing, but I learned that we can meet even the hardest challenges if we take them one small step at a time.

58

*Even the tiniest spark can
reignite the fire of love.*

When Raymond and Marion came to our workshop, they were on the verge of divorce. They had been living apart for two months, but even this separation wasn't enough to soften the pain and anger that had been accumulating between them for nearly four years. Raymond worked for a high-powered law firm that demanded absolute loyalty and faithful service from its employees. This translated into big bucks, but it also wreaked havoc on the personal lives of the staff attorneys, most of whom were either single or divorced. As Raymond himself had admitted, "This place is about as good for marriage as cigarette smoke is for your lungs." It was not a pretty picture. Over the six-year period that Raymond had worked for the firm, he had seen "more marriages than I can keep track of crash and burn."

Not only was the job intensely demanding, but because many of his clients were out of town there was a great deal of traveling involved. Raymond, unlike many of his associates, was able to resist the temptation to engage in dalliances when he was on the road. But when he came home, he would often be so exhausted from his travels that he had little energy left for Marion or their two children. Their marriage was deteriorating from chronic neglect and emotional disconnection. After months of conflict and separation, they were dangling over the precipice of divorce.

In a relationship workshop, Marion was surprised when we suggested that since she was the one experiencing the most pain, it was up to her to take a more active role in strengthening the marriage. Our advice was not because she was any more responsible than Raymond for the quality of their relationship, but because she was more motivated to change it due to her level of acute distress. Raymond's workaholism had numbed him to Marion's pain and to his own hidden pain from being so disconnected from his family. Even though Marion felt like it wasn't fair for her to have to be the one to always initiate work on the relationship, she realized that until Raymond awoke from his work-induced trance, there was little possibility that things between them would ever change. She knew that if there was any chance of salvaging the marriage, she would have to step into a leadership role, and that even if she did there was no guarantee.

She left the workshop promising herself that she would put her best efforts into making things work and would take responsibility for facilitating the process of creating a marriage that she knew they both really wanted. She embraced this commitment, working to continually push her doubts and fears into the background. She held fast to a vision that they could get the substance and depth back again, operating from a conviction that this troubled time was only temporary. Although Raymond was pessimistic about salvaging their marriage and often felt like it would be simpler and easier to "just cut our losses and move on," Marion knew there was still a spark left. She was not yet ready to declare her marriage dead as long as there was still a breath of life in it.

Slowly, as her conviction grew stronger, Raymond became increasingly open to the possibility that things might work out between them. As Marion focused more on her intention to bring more love and appreciation into their marriage, the frequency of her complaints to Raymond diminished, and he found himself more able to open to her and feel her love, instead of her resentment and irritation. Because she was focusing on what she really wanted to experience with her husband rather than on how he was disappointing her, Raymond felt much more inclined to spend more time with his family.

They took a weeklong vacation together, without the children, something they had not done in several years. They reinstituted date-night and retained a regularly scheduled babysitter. Raymond took the risk of taking a stand with his immediate supervisor about the business trips he was willing to accept, and surprisingly his supervisor agreed to modify his schedule.

Together they breathed life into and resuscitated a previously dying marriage. In the process of working together, love began to pour back into their hearts and transformed their relationship. "Looking back," said Marion, "our marriage had a near-death experience. But it was because we saw how close to the edge we really were that we were able to muster the effort to bring it back to life." Like survivors who come back from death's door, Marion and Raymond now have a greater appreciation for each other than they ever had before. They are both certain that they will never get that close to the edge again.

59

If you find out what your partner wants and help them get it, you'll both be happier.

Seth was an engineer and a very concrete thinker. The world of feelings and emotions was foreign to him. He didn't know his wife Lillah's deepest desires, nor even his own; he didn't ask those kinds of questions. Although he loved Lillah, he didn't really know her. They had been living out a script they'd adopted years ago, and they had never stopped to find out whether it truly suited their individual and shared needs and desires. After a particularly painful argument, it became apparent to each of them that they had been living like emotional strangers. Rather than seek a divorce, though, they decided to find out who they each were really living with. Their inquiry began with some very basic questions: What do you dislike? How do you like to spend your free time?

What do you enjoy doing with me? What do you need when you're unhappy? What kind of support works for you? What turns you on? What turns you off? What do you really love to do? What brings you the greatest joy?

One of the first things they discovered was a shared desire to spice up their sex life. When they began bringing more play and creativity into the bedroom, they were off to a good start. Then Lillah shared that she wanted them to own their own home. Within a year they managed to come up with a down payment. Seth wanted to plant fruit trees and bulbs. Lillah didn't care much for working in the yard, but she spent time keeping her husband company while he dug and planted, because it meant so much to him. They both found that when they helped each other to fulfill their desires, it never felt like a sacrifice, and they could share the pleasure together. These two were quick studies, and their relationship became a gratifying exploration of how they could gift each other with the wonderful longings of their hearts. They came to realize that what they most desired was to bring more love into their lives. They learned to create the conditions that give rise to openhearted living.

They had been practicing for months when Seth was offered an engineering assignment overseas. Accepting the assignment meant that Lillah would be left alone for eight weeks, with three spirited children plus her job. Already overextended, she knew this was going to be tough. Seth was going to be in locations where he wouldn't be able to have phone contact. Lillah saw this as a final exam. She knew how much Seth wanted to go, and she didn't hesitate to support his decision. Although there were some difficult aspects of the separation, it turned out to be enormously enriching. Lillah found that when put to the test, she could handle life's demands. She was rewarded with a greater sense of pride and trust in herself as well as Seth's deep appreciation and respect.

60

Marriage alone does not make you a better person, but accepting its challenges does.

LINDA: When I got married, I was weak, wimpy, unconscious, and inexperienced. I had no idea what I was getting into, and I was filled with unrealistic fantasies. I had swallowed Hollywood's romantic myths whole. Over time, my life experience helped me to awaken from this trance. It wasn't always fun or easy — myths die hard — but eventually, I wised up. In the early seventies, I remember seeing a life-size poster of Swami Satchidananda in a loincloth, crouched down on a surfboard. The caption read, "You can't stop the waves from coming, but you can learn to surf."

Marriage, I learned, is like that. Even when you are a skilled surfer, you still get knocked around by the waves. The challenges just keep coming. I got tossed around plenty while I was learning. Everyone does. Eventually it got easier, especially when I realized that marriage can be a path — a practice for becoming a stronger, more whole person. Then the challenges became: What am I supposed to be learning here? How can I develop myself more fully? What are the gifts that I can give?

One of the things it took me a while to learn was that focusing on what Charlie was doing and trying to change him was not a good strategy for bringing fulfillment into my life. As I became more able to concentrate on myself rather than Charlie, I began to experience a greater return on my energy output. Rather than trying to get Charlie to take better care of me, I focused more on doing that myself. It was a much more efficient way of doing things, like taking out the middleman. In addition, it helped me to develop in ways that I really wanted to. My levels of courage, self-discipline, honesty, patience, self-trust, forgiveness, balance, and compassion all grew. I had my hands full!

The marriage served up lots of growth opportunities. I experienced and worked through anxiety about money, conflict over child-rearing concerns, loneliness that resulted from physical or emotional separation from Charlie, anger over feeling unappreciated, disappointed expectations (too many to list), panic in the face of serious illness, and frustration about not having enough time for all the pieces of my life. The acceptance of what my marriage has handed me has powerfully catalyzed my growth into a more conscious, decent, loving person.

In addressing the Explorer Club, the organization that funded his first unsuccessful trip to the summit of Mt. Everest, Sir Edmund Hillary turned to a projected photo of the mountain, shook his fist, and shouted, "You can't get any bigger, but I can." Hillary did indeed go back and conquer that mountain; he got bigger. For him, that meant developing to a greater degree the qualities necessary to meet the challenges of Everest. Marriage invites us to do the same — it challenges us to get bigger. Marriage may not always provide us with the partner of our dreams, but if we open fully to what it calls forth from us, we will become the partner of our dreams.

We've all known couples that have been married for years but haven't seemed to learn much about life and loving. They may still be closed, fearful, angry, resentful, and negative. These couples may endure, but without taking advantage of life's teachable moments. All they have to show for their marriages is the time they have logged together. Other couples have wisdom far beyond the years they've spent together. They've used the challenges of their individual lives, as well as those served up by the marriage, as opportunities to learn and grow. Anyone, at any time, can accept the challenges that continually present themselves, rather than avoid them. In the acceptance of the challenges, compassion, wisdom, and love mature.

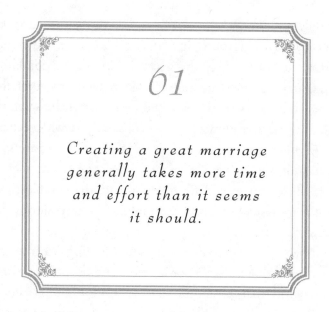

61

*Creating a great marriage
generally takes more time
and effort than it seems
it should.*

One of our favorite Bob Dylan lyrics is "He who isn't busy being born is busy dying." These words speak to the challenge of creating a vibrant life. This same stance is also required to promote vitality in a marriage. Failing to do so will dry up the passion that originally fired our desires for each other. When this occurs, conditioned patterns may overtake the relationship and erode the foundation of love. Over time, little things that we try to overlook or set aside can accumulate, and we find ourselves filled with frustration and disappointment. Unmet needs and denied resentment can destroy a relationship that was previously strong and healthy. We might wake up one day to find that we are overwhelmed by hopelessness. If we are not conscious, aware, and vigilant, our relationship can self-destruct.

Loving relationships can't be rushed. It requires time and effort to make a relationship a beautiful creation. And it takes continued work to keep that relationship in good condition. It may take years to develop a style of being together that works well for both people. The best relationships are the ones that are ever growing, being constantly, newly created.

Another wise sage of our time, Woody Allen, once said, "A relationship is like a shark; if it doesn't keep moving, it dies." Because we tend to underestimate the complexity of human relations, we expect deep fulfillment to come quickly and easily. This belief sets up the inevitability of great disappointment, along with the likelihood of feeling either resentment (toward our partner) or inadequacy (toward our selves). In a world that promotes the expectation of immediate gratification, it's easy to forget that most of us enter marriage not yet having fully mastered the art of being a loving and authentic human being. The many facets of marriage furnish us with the experience necessary to finish the job. This is the work of a lifetime, not an overnight endeavor. It usually takes more patience and faith than we realize to sustain the effort without giving up in frustration. When both partners are willing to share fully in this process, concern about time fades into the background, as we become entranced by the joy of the process.

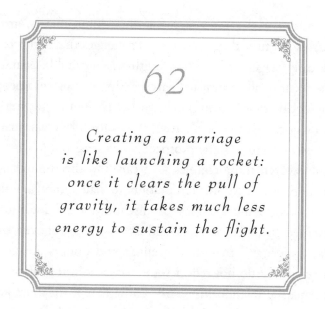

62

*Creating a marriage
is like launching a rocket:
once it clears the pull of
gravity, it takes much less
energy to sustain the flight.*

Just as a space shuttle burns about 90 percent of its fuel during the initial moments of its flight, marriage requires its greatest expenditure of energy during its early stages. In marriage, however, these stages are more likely to last a few years rather than a few minutes. It's at the beginning of most marriages that we are likely to encounter the real challenges of commitment, such as the need to let go of control, the ability to overcome resistance to change, the willingness to put aside our ego-desires in favor of shared concerns, and the willingness to be vulnerable and honest in the face of fear and pain.

Fortunately, this degree of concentrated energy is not required on a permanent basis. Once a marriage gets past the initial stages, the amount of energy needed to fuel the commitment decreases significantly. Unfortunately, many couples fail to make it past those challenges that show up in the early stages. When faced with the inevitable demands that occur in all committed partnerships, one or both people may decide that it's too much work; that they're just not up for the job; that they can't live this way for fifty years; that in one way or another, the prospect is overwhelming.

However, those couples who can find the strength and the hope to resist the temptation to bail out when they hit the inevitable feelings of discouragement are usually rewarded for their stamina and efforts. They are the ones who understand that these feelings and doubts are nearly universal and do not reflect some basic dysfunction in their new marital relationship. They know that if they just keep trying, and trusting, they will in all likelihood develop the strength that marriage demands. Just as an athlete grows stronger by facing down his desire to quit and by hanging in there when his body wants to give up, committed partners do the same. The reward for this kind of perseverance is more than a good marriage; it's also the almost overwhelming sense of personal well-being that is the by-product of honoring the marital commitment. Yes, it can be damn hard, but the process gets easier over time, and the rewards can greatly exceed our expectations.

63

*Being attracted to someone
else doesn't diminish the
quality of your marriage;
acting on that attraction does.*

LINDA: I'm a recovering jealous wife. In the early days of our marriage, I was horribly insecure. One time, when I saw Charlie dancing at a party with a tall, slender, attractive blond, I slipped into a bad case of resentment. On the drive home I exploded. There was a terrible scene, and we almost got into an accident. After the dust settled, we were able to discuss his flirtatiousness and my reactivity to it. Over the years there have been other episodes like this one, and I gradually came to trust that Charlie's flirting is harmless, nothing that would put our relationship at risk. No longer possessed by panic at these times, I now find myself merely observant.

It has, however, taken time and conversation and adjustment on both our parts to get to this point. I know that neither of us would knowingly do anything to jeopardize our marriage or hurt the other — our boundaries are clear. At ease in this certainty, I can rejoice in the aliveness of the human spirit, which is what leads us both to feel the spark of attraction to others from time to time. It doesn't mean that there is anything missing or wrong with our marriage just because we occasionally experience an attraction — sometimes even an intense one — to another person. Feelings in the body, thoughts tickling the mind, fantasies in the imagination are just part of the passing show. They come, and if we don't feed them, they go. They're a testimonial that our passion is alive and well.

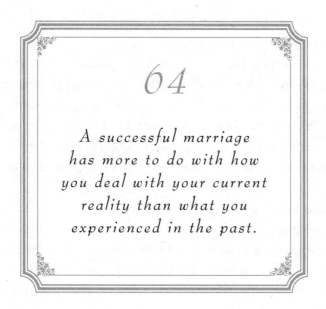

64

*A successful marriage
has more to do with how
you deal with your current
reality than what you
experienced in the past.*

As therapists, you would think we would be the last people to say that the past isn't all that important. But we've learned a lot from our clients, many of whom have spent years telling and retelling the stories of their childhood. While there is no doubt that early life experience plays a significant role in shaping the people we become, it's clear that other factors exert even greater influence on the quality of our current lives and relationships. We can assess, dissect, evaluate, and analyze the past for the rest of our lives, and many of us do. We may use stories from the past to justify a belief in the inevitability of unhappiness in our lives. Such storytelling in itself will have very little impact on the process of shaping our future. Learning from the past, and putting those lessons into practice in the present, is what brings about a different future. This process requires us to examine and question our long-held or hidden beliefs.

No matter how often a woman reminds herself of how abusive her father was and attributes her mistrust of men to him, her relationships will not change until she learns the lessons, painful though they may be, that are inherent in recovering from a traumatic experience. It's not enough to remember the past; we need to integrate its lessons into our current lives in order for the future to be different. This means learning more about our own part in our failed relationships and identifying alternatives that we may have been too frightened or confused to recognize at the time. We'll know that we are making progress when we no longer need to retell the same old stories and when we find ourselves taking new and more effective actions in our relationships. With gentleness and respect, we can slow down the film of our lives to allow the old feelings to surface, and in the process, find the strength and wisdom that we need to make choices that will enhance our lives.

In order for it to thrive,
love requires separateness
as well as togetherness.

LINDA: When I was a little girl, we would sometimes play a game called the three-legged race. I'd pair up with another girl, an adult would tie two of our legs together with a bandanna, and we would hobble along, racing against other teams. We couldn't move very quickly, but we got to laugh a lot. The pair that crossed the finish line first got the prize. I always loved this game, even though I rarely won.

Many couples apply this model to marriage. They try to do everything together and engage in few activities that are not shared. This kind of extreme togetherness usually isn't a sign of love but rather of a mutual dependency that often breeds hidden resentment. While this arrangement often seems to work in the early stages of marriage, it's only a matter of time before it breaks down. What initially felt like security, comfort, and closeness begins to feel like control, suffocation, and entrapment. Separateness is as essential to any relationship as togetherness is. When either aspect is missing, the relationship will be unbalanced and possibly unstable. For a marriage to thrive, each person has to be secure within their own life and be responsive and connected to their partner.

While we're on our own, we have the chance to feel our uniqueness, express our separate tastes, and move at our own pace and rhythm. In addition, while we're out there having those experiences, our partner has a chance to miss us and we both get to have a fond reunion when we come back. Instead of two slices attempting to join into being a whole, we learn to maintain our autonomy and engage fully as two distinct human beings.

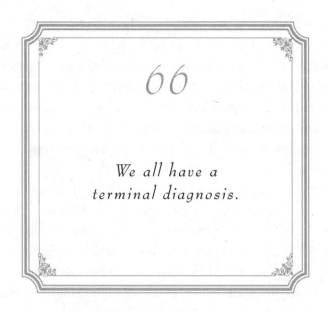

We all have a
terminal diagnosis.

Mollie and Shepherd met when they were both fifteen. They fell in love and dated all through high school. When they graduated, Shepherd decided he wanted to experience being with other women, and they broke up. After two months of attempting to stay apart, they both felt miserable and got back together. They got married, and the first few years went well. They rarely fought and when they did they usually settled it quickly. They were generally honest, respectful, and kind with each other. They shared numerous interests and expressed their affection frequently and openly. It was almost too good to be true.

When asked about the secret of their success, Mollie explained that she had developed kidney disease when she was a small child. She was one of the early experimental kidney transplant recipients and had to take medication every day to ensure that her body didn't reject the kidney. There was no way of knowing how long she would survive. Mollie and Shepherd continuously lived with the specter of death. This awareness had a profound impact on all of their choices, large and small. They were able to let go of many little concerns because they had truly learned not to sweat the small stuff.

Mollie and Shepherd knew something that most of us tend to forget: our time together is limited and we don't know when it will be up. In this sense, we all have a terminal diagnosis. The awareness that death is inevitable and that one day we may no longer have our beloved mate in our life puts our day-to-day events in perspective. Although many of us prefer not to think of such "depressing" matters, bringing this understanding to mind actually enlightens us with feelings of gratitude, appreciation, and urgency. Although we don't need to hurry through our lives, we also don't need to waste time. In denying the inevitability of death, our own and our partner's, we reinforce the illusion that we have all the time in the world. We are lulled into the false notion that we can afford to put off what truly matters for yet another day. Very few people reach the end of their lives feeling that they spent too much time being loving and openhearted. Quite a few, however, regret delaying, or never sharing at all, their expressions of love, gratitude, and openness.

When we find the courage to accept the truth of our existence — that it is limited and temporary — it becomes impossible to live in a state of denial and delay. Although many people felt sorry for Mollie and Shepherd because her illness prevented them from living a "normal" life, they each felt that they were blessed — not only because of the love that they shared, but because fate had made it impossible for them to ever forget the most important truth of their lives: that we don't have a moment to lose to show our love; for this they each felt the deepest gratitude.

*Don't keep feelings of
gratitude to yourself.*

How often does your sense of gratitude disappear before you share it with your partner? In this case, "if you just ignore it, it will pass" is unfortunately true. When we fail to share outwardly what we feel inwardly, the feeling soon dissipates, and an opportunity to deepen our relationship is lost. One of the easiest and most potent ways of strengthening your connection is to voice your feelings of appreciation and gratitude. Acknowledgment of any type, no matter how insignificant it may seem, can deepen the bond of caring far more than we realize.

Consider for a moment all those times that you are reminded of something about your partner that you appreciate, but you don't express it. Perhaps she prepared a delicious meal or listened to your concerns and frustrations about a problem at work. Maybe you watched in admiration of how patiently he helped your son with his homework assignment, or you noticed the extra care she took to nurture the plants or pets, or you were touched by his willingness to get up in the middle of the night with the baby. Maybe she brought you a cup of tea, rubbed your sore shoulders at the end of a particularly demanding workday, or let you decide which movie to see. Simple things like keeping our partner company while they wash the dishes remind them that they are loved. Not a single day should pass without sharing gratitude for something. Every acknowledgment is a gift to ourselves as well as our partner, since the goodwill that it promotes ultimately comes back to us many times over.

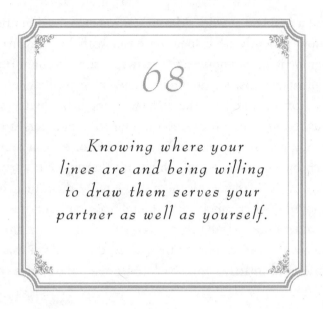

68

Knowing where your lines are and being willing to draw them serves your partner as well as yourself.

LINDA: One day, back in the early seventies, a group of my women friends and I were sitting around complaining bitterly about one of our favorite subjects, the selfishness of men. "With all that male privilege they've been raised with, they expect to have things their way. Down with the patriarchy! Men are such babies, so self-centered, so immature, so selfish!" We agreed that men were the basic problem, and that something should be done about them. A few days later I walked into the bathroom to find the toilet seat up. I was tempted to express my outrage over yet another example of male selfishness, but in a moment of realization I decided to keep my mouth shut. I thought to myself, "There are things that are worth taking a stand over, but this isn't one of them."

Several years ago, Charlie and I agreed to go on a date together every week. When we first set this up, he would often cancel it or arrive late, cutting back the time we had together. I knew that unlike the toilet seat this was something I was unwilling to overlook or compromise on. Without threatening him or yelling, I took a clear stand, affirming to Charlie how important this agreement was to me and how much I cherished every minute we got to spend together. Our weekly date became an established part of our lives. These few hours have become the highlight of my week, enriching and fulfilling us both. Charlie has thanked me many times for holding my ground on this issue. These days, we rarely miss a date. When we do, it's often I who does the canceling, and we always reschedule. Some issues matter more than others. I'll save my energy for those that do.

69

*You don't have to be able
to love well to get married;
the training occurs
on the job.*

CHARLIE: I was twenty-five when Linda and I got married, a very young twenty-five. It's a good thing that I had no idea what I was in for, because if I had I would have headed for parts unknown instead of showing up at the wedding. It wasn't that I was more mature than my friends, most of whom were single; I was just too unconscious to appreciate the real challenges and responsibility inherent in marriage.

Within two years of our marriage I was a father, the sole provider of our household with a job, and a full-time graduate student. Consumed with doubts about my ability to handle what I felt was an insurmountable challenge, I was overwhelmed. As a young person I had promised myself that when I grew up I would be a great husband and an even greater father. I was going to give my family everything that

I had wanted to receive but hadn't when I was growing up — a loving, fun-filled, supportive, secure, and comfortable home. As a parent and husband I found myself falling into the same patterns of isolation, anger, irritability, and overwork that I had observed in my father and sworn I would never repeat. I was angry and frustrated with myself because I was failing to fulfill the most important commitment of my life. On more than one occasion I packed my bags, convinced that I just wasn't made out of the right stuff for marriage. For some reason, I never left. In the process of hanging in there, I eventually came to more fully develop the strength, the patience, the love, and the commitment that marriage requires. But I didn't just "get it." It came over time and was a slow, gradual, and often frustrating process. What I couldn't see as a twenty-five-year-old was that it was okay that I wasn't yet "fully cooked," that if I just hung in there and did my work, the experience itself would eventually grow me up. And it did.

It is just as possible to make the mistake of waiting too long to commit to a relationship as it is to jump in too soon. What is often viewed as commitment phobia may actually be more a matter of wanting to wait until we have the maturity and strength to be the kind of partner that we want to be. But this approach is somewhat akin to the idea of trying to learn how to ride a bicycle before you actually get on it. The skill only becomes developed in the process of doing it. Unfortunately, this means that we won't be able to avoid the stumbles that are inevitable in the early stages of the learning process. Those who are unwilling to risk falling never learn to ride. No amount of preparation, workshops, therapy, books, or self-help tapes will be sufficient to prevent the breakdowns that the development of the capacity to love requires. We don't become a loving partner prior to getting married; we bring our unfinished, un-grown-up self to the marriage and finish the job there. If you wait until you're ready, you never will be.

70

Privacy won't hurt your marriage, but secrecy will.

Flo was in business for herself. She had no established financial credit because of debts in her previous marriage. Occasionally, her husband Monte allowed her to use his credit card, but when her business hit a slump she used it on several occasions without his knowledge and ran up a large bill. Flo expected her business profits to soon begin flowing, so that she would be able to pay off the account without Monte ever finding out. Each month, she would intercept the statements from the credit card company before Monte could see them. Things didn't go as planned when one day after four months, the bank called Monte about the account. When he got the news, he became enraged. There had been many previous incidents where

Flo had concealed information from him about money. This was the last straw. "You lied to me again," Monte screamed at her when he found out. "I can't trust you!" Monte was not interested in Flo's attempts to justify her actions; he had already made up his mind. They never rebuilt the broken trust.

The problem was not that Flo failed to reveal the details of her business to Monte. She never had, and he didn't expect her to. She had had difficult seasons in her business before, and he neither needed nor wanted to hear all of the details of her professional challenges. Her business was her business, and the particulars of her work situation were in the realm of privacy. What was different about this situation was that she deliberately withheld information in order to protect herself. Her actions were motivated by a desire to conceal the truth from Monte.

Secrets are information that we deliberately withhold in order to allow others to believe something that isn't true. While we may claim we are doing this for the benefit of others, generally our motivation is to protect ourselves from others' reactions. Concealing the truth, regardless of the motivation, is like a smoldering fire that slowly burns away the trust that holds a relationship together.

The desire for privacy is different from secrecy. It comes from the intention to establish boundaries between our personal and shared space. Privacy is necessary to promote the kind of separateness required to develop our sense of self. Used for this purpose, privacy can support us to bring more of ourselves to all of our relationships because it helps strengthen who we are. Privacy expands; secrecy contracts. There is a great depth of trust that comes in knowing that nothing of relevance and importance to the relationship will be concealed. This trust is the foundation on which great marriages are built.

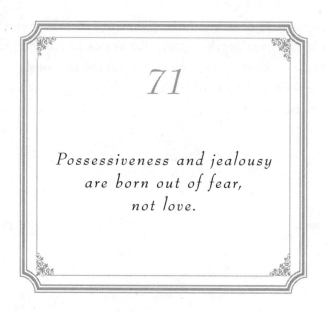

71

Possessiveness and jealousy
are born out of fear,
not love.

LINDA: Early in our marriage I was frequently consumed with feelings of jealousy and possessiveness. I experienced recurring bouts with self-doubt and lived in perpetual fear of losing Charlie to someone else. This fear caused me to try to control him. My efforts only served to push him further away, leaving me in a vicious cycle. The more I tried to get reassurance from him, the more he pulled back. I was jealous of his friends and I felt threatened by his connections to his colleagues at work. I felt competitive with the books that he spent so much time reading, with his guitar, even with his motorcycle. I saw them all as things that were taking him away from me. He was as focused on his own life as I was on our life together. The more "we" I tried to be, the more "me" he seemed to become.

Eventually, I came to see that I was going to have to do something about my jealousy or I would lose my sanity as well as my marriage. I knew that my possessiveness arose out of the same insecurities that had plagued me since childhood. My attempts to extract reassurance from Charlie didn't help, even when I managed to succeed in getting it from him; I never felt satisfied because it wasn't freely given. The roots of my jealousy were fear — fear of loss, fear of loneliness, fear of being helpless, fear of being unloved, fear of being abandoned, fear of not being good enough . . . it was a long list.

As uncomfortable as it felt to become aware of all of this, there was something liberating about finally seeing my part in it. I saw that I couldn't control Charlie, but I could control the way I responded to my fear and insecurity. I learned to bring compassion and patience to myself, and to give myself the loving attention I had been trying to get from him. I reminded myself that I had made it through difficulty and loss before, that I was a survivor and could be again if need be. Slowly I grew into a more self-confident woman, and found the strength in myself that I had sought from Charlie. Meanwhile, he became more attentive to me when I stopped trying to extract attention from him.

I still experience attacks of jealousy, but they're infrequent and short-lived. Most of the time I handle them on my own without having to even speak about them with Charlie. Generally he isn't even aware of them. I don't act out the fear as I once did, with whining demands or bids for his attention. Sometimes it seems like a miracle, but I know that my effort, patience, and persistence have been the real factors in the transformative process of growing myself up.

72

Facing your fears builds strength; avoiding them diminishes it.

The more we withdraw from challenges, the more fearful we become. The problem with avoidance is that the underlying issues don't get resolved. Fear doesn't grow unless it's fed. Whenever we encounter a difficult situation, there is the possibility of deepening our fear through avoidance or diminishing it by facing what we are afraid of. The outcome of our actions may be less important than whether or not we confront the situation. The greatest failure is the failure to face the truth.

Rita and Mimi were a lesbian couple. They were both avoiders. Neither could bear to bring up concerns that might be disturbing. Rita grew up in a chaotic family where conflict almost always led to physical or emotional violence. More often than not, she found herself on the receiving end.

She learned to protect herself by keeping her mouth shut and going along with what she thought was expected of her. Mimi grew up in a family where no one ever spoke above a whisper. "My family was so quiet," Mimi said one day, "that they made the morgue sound rowdy." Not only did she never witness her parents fighting, she never even saw a minor disagreement. If they ever did argue, it was behind closed doors. She grew up believing that arguments were wrong and scary. They must be dangerous, she concluded, since her parents would do anything rather than fight, even drink addictively and endure major depression.

It wasn't, however, the past that was destroying Mimi and Rita's relationship. It was the current reality of a shared conspiracy to avoid expressing feelings to each other. Rita and Mimi felt the normal hurts, disappointments, frustrations, and grievances that all couples feel from time to time. The problem was that neither ever acknowledged them. The more they withheld, the more fearful they became. This bred more withholding. Eventually their relationship deteriorated into a wasteland of resentment. When they finally felt they had nothing to lose, they came to relationship counseling wanting to find out if there was anything left to salvage.

Together they began the excruciatingly difficult task of breaking patterns of denial and avoidance that had been present in each of their families for generations. They struggled with their own fears of conflict, as well as the fears of the parents, grandparents, and beyond who had passed this pattern on to their children. If it weren't for Mimi and Rita's desire not to inflict this pattern on their own daughter, they would almost certainly have been unmotivated to take on this huge challenge. Their love for her prompted them to find the courage to finally speak openly to each other. At first, a painful level of anxiety filled their conversations. Both Mimi and Rita felt certain that the violation of their families' unspoken rules of denial would result in unbearable suffering and grave punishment. But gradually the opposite proved to be the case. With each encounter, they both became less fearful and more courageous.

Courage isn't the absence of fear; it's the willingness to act in the face of fear from a deeper commitment. Rita and Mimi both had this commitment. Although it was born out of their love for their daughter, in time it took root in the love for themselves and each other. Their willingness to confront their own fear liberated them from what had only recently been the paralyzing grip of the past.

73

*Authenticity is contagious
and habit-forming.*

Ashley and Dylan were newly in love. One day, on a mountain hike, they came to a waterfall and pools of melted snow.
"Let's go swimming," Dylan impulsively suggested. Ashley
thought, "Are you crazy?" but she wanted so badly to impress
Dylan with her adventurousness that she took off all of her
clothes and plunged headfirst into the water. The icy cold
slammed into her body, but she covered her pain by plaster-
ing a frozen grin on her face. She even floated around to create the impression that she was enjoying the experience. In
reality, her limbs were beginning to numb from the early
stages of hypothermia. Dylan watched in amazement. He
began to undress and poked one toe into the water. "Too
cold for me," he said. "I'm not going in." Ashley was
shocked. She quickly got out of the water feeling angry with

Dylan and simultaneously grudgingly acknowledging him for his willingness to be real. His honesty illuminated her hidden desire to please him, and she felt foolish and embarrassed by her phony heroics.

Ashley learned an important lesson that day. She became aware of how frequently she had chosen to make herself into someone other than who she was. After this powerful experience, she often made a different choice. She came to see how often she tended to be inauthentic, and through her self-observation saw what she was giving up of herself in order to be more accepted. "Be yourself; don't pretend to be other than who you are" became her guideline. That one experience taught her that being secure in who you are allows you to be yourself without the need to prove anything. Personal authenticity often inspires others to be real too.

74

Don't say anything about your partner that you're not willing to say to them.

Jenna felt that she was doing almost all of the housework, and that Clayton expected to be pampered. She was angry that he spent so much time with the guys, playing ball, watching the games, and hanging out. She didn't feel that Clayton made decisions with her, but more often than not decided things on his own. But she was too frightened to bring these issues up directly to Clayton. Jenna spent a lot of time complaining about Clayton to her women friends. Her friends were supportive, offering stories that reaffirmed their shared beliefs about how they were all victimized by their selfish, immature, and insensitive men. "They all just want it their way. Men are so selfish. Men are egoed out, so self-centered. They are such little boys. They don't have a clue."

Such comments were commonplace in their private conversations. There wasn't a single time when a friend was responsible in her level of support and said anything like, "I think you should talk that over with Clayton and straighten it out." All this so-called support kept their marriage stuck.

Jenna's sister-in-law was present at one of the women's bashing fests. Out of concern for both Clayton and Jenna, she told her husband about the remarks Jenna had made about Clayton being selfish. Clayton's brother called Clayton and repeated what he had heard. "Your wife calls you a selfish, uncaring jerk who takes her for granted. Is this true about you? What's up? Are you two having trouble?" As soon as he could recover from the shock of this news, Clayton said, "I thought things were going along just fine. I'm making every effort to be a good husband. I had better see if there is something going on I don't know about."

He immediately went to confront his wife. He wasn't angry as much as bewildered and hurt. "What is this I hear? Are you talking trash about me to your friends, about my being a lousy husband? Is that what you really think of me? Do you think I'm a lousy, selfish husband?" When he confronted her, she could see how hurt he was. She didn't deny his accusations. She felt like a coward for spreading terrible, exaggerated judgments. She didn't get defensive. In an instant, Jenna realized that she had been playing out the same pattern that she had seen in her own family growing up. Her mom had repeatedly spoken to her and whoever else would listen about what a disappointment her dad had been. Jenna remembered how awkward she had felt hearing her father discredited. She remembered how desperately she had wished that they would speak to each other and work out their problems and not tell her about them. She was just a little girl and couldn't fix these adult problems.

She told Clayton the truth. "I feel terrible. I feel so guilty about talking behind your back. I've been thoughtless and unfair. I hope that one day you will forgive me for talking badly about you. I will break this old pattern. You'll see." And, true to her word, as soon as she noticed herself tempted to begin speaking to her women friends in a derogatory way about him, she made a mental note to go to him at the first possible moment. She drew up her courage to speak directly to him. She told him about how exploited she felt, being in charge of all the housework, and that they had to work out an agreement around shopping, cooking, dishes, vacuuming, and laundry. She spoke honestly about wanting to be re-assured that she was as important to him as his guy friends. When she met with the fear and resistance inside herself, she noticed the urge to slide back into her old complaining habit. But she was unwilling to repeat the past and settle for the broken-down wreck of a marriage that her parents had lived in.

Several conversations were required to establish new habits. But most of their thorny dilemmas eventually did get worked out. Even though some of the discussions were heated and difficult, at least Jenna no longer felt like a dirty sneak. Over time, there was nothing that was off-limits to speak about. These days, neither of them can bear withhold-ing strong feelings, good or bad, for even short periods of time, and they always go first to each other when there's something to say.

Once Jenna stopped complaining to her friends, she didn't hear them complaining so much anymore either. Maybe they got the message too.

75

Your greatest weakness
can become your
greatest strength.

LINDA: For years, one of my greatest weaknesses was my tendency to see myself as a victim. Just before my youngest child began school, I was passionate about doing something more substantial with my career. I had put my work on hold for several years and felt like a racehorse at the starting gate, bursting to be set free. At the same time, however, I felt fearful about making such a big change. This inner tension expressed itself outwardly in the form of conflict with Charlie. Feeling like a long-suffering martyr, I accused him of holding me back from the kind of life I wanted to live. He was deeply involved with his career, and I felt that the children needed to have at least one parent around. My position was somewhat reasonable, but I had blown it out of proportion. I was working myself into a state of deep bitterness about not getting the kind of support that I needed to take the next step. When I was able to back away from the situation and take a more honest look, I saw how frightened I was of moving ahead. I wasn't sure that I was going to be able to succeed professionally. I feared that the children would suffer in my absence, and I worried that there might not be enough time left for Charlie and me. Eventually, this view gave way to the realization that Charlie was not my enemy. My real enemies were the doubt, confusion, and fear within myself that I hadn't yet resolved.

This lesson is one that I have had to learn a number of times. When I am tempted to point the bony finger of blame at others, I remind myself that this pattern of thinking and behaving has caused me emotional pain, and I remember my motivation for strengthening this weak area. I still hear the inner voice saying things like "he is the problem," but I no longer allow the words to come flying out my mouth. I know that I need to find out what is really going on inside myself. When I do, I usually discover that there is a level of personal responsibility that I am avoiding. Then I ask myself how I might be responsible, rather than continuing to project blame onto others. My recovery from victim consciousness has contributed to the development of inner strength that has impacted every aspect of my life. The petty gratification of feeling like a victim pales in comparison to the sense of self-worth and self-respect that have come from growing up.

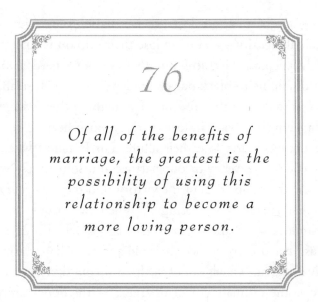

76

Of all of the benefits of marriage, the greatest is the possibility of using this relationship to become a more loving person.

"At the end of life," writes Jack Kornfield, "our questions are very simple: Did I live fully? Did I love well?"[*] Marriage is a perfect training ground for the heart. Blessedly, by learning to truly love one person, we become more able to express love to, and receive love from, all people — and all of life, the whole universe, all that *is.*

The more we see the wonder of what marriage offers us, the more we can allow it to grow us and open us deeply and fully. And the more fully we open our hearts and minds and experience profound connection with another being, the easier it becomes to resist passing and distracting temptations. The desire to be right, to look good, to accumulate

---

[*] Jack Kornfield, *A Grateful Heart,* ed. M. J. Ryan (Berkeley: Conari Press, 1994), p. 123.

things, to be in control, to receive praise, recognition, and external security — all these lose their grip on us and eventually fall away. It turns out that we don't need a lot of self-discipline to break our compulsive patterns. Instead, we need to focus on the creation of something that is far *more* compelling — living in love, with an open heart. Then the competing desires lose their allure. For instance, when we struggle for power with our partner and sometimes "win," we feel the hollowness of the victory, and then we gradually put less energy into chasing it. When two people share a commitment to make their marriage a vehicle for inner transformation, they shed their old and petty habits as naturally as a snake crawls out of its dried-up old skin. And so we receive the ultimate gift of marriage — the opportunity to heighten our capacity to experience joy, gratitude, and fulfillment and to become a more deeply loving human being.

77

If your partner thinks
something is important, it is!

CHARLIE: "You're making a mountain out of a molehill!" is a sentence that has done massive damage to countless relationships, including ours. It used to be my standard response to any of Linda's concerns that I didn't take as seriously as she did. While I usually insisted that I was only trying to help her to put things in perspective, somehow this never seemed to comfort her very much. Perhaps that's because the implicit message in this statement is "I know better than you do what really matters, and if you don't believe me I'll explain to you why you're wrong." My insistence that I was "only trying to help," and that she was ungrateful, made things even worse. Predictably, both of us ended up feeling misunderstood and unappreciated. The pattern continued for years and was the source of enormous frustration. Instead of feeling supported by me, Linda often felt criticized and judged by my words.

The truth was that I was frustrated with myself. I hated seeing Linda feeling upset or hurt. I felt helpless and inadequate when I thought that I couldn't do anything to make her feel better. Trying to get her to dismiss her feelings was my way of avoiding what was going on inside me. My true intention had little to do with helping Linda; I was trying to make myself feel less uncomfortable. Despite my insistence to the contrary, Linda sensed my real motivation, and that is what she responded to.

It wasn't until we could get to the bottom of what was going on with each of us that we could break this pattern, and I could finally begin deeply listening to her. That is all she really wanted from me — just to listen, not try to change the way she was feeling.

Now I know that if I don't see why something is such a big deal to Linda, it's not her problem. I know that what she needs from me is just to hear her out, not to fix things for her. When I believe that it's my job to see to it that Linda is always happy, then I'm less likely to be open to hearing her grievances and complaints. Remembering that Linda's happiness isn't my responsibility makes it much easier for me to hear her concerns. What a relief to know that even if I can't change the situation that's upsetting to her, I can always give her what she most needs in the moment — my full and loving attention.

78

*Marriages never outgrow
the need for romance.*

One of the greatest hazards of marriage is the tendency for the drudgery of daily living to displace the deeper purpose of the relationship. There's no denying the need to manage the material and financial responsibilities of a family. The challenge is to keep these concerns in their place so they don't weigh so heavily upon us that they drown out the voice that reflects our deeper needs and longings. One of the ways to maintain the kind of perspective that nourishes our heart, as well as our hearth, is to keep romance alive.

Romance is more than candlelight and flowers; it's a quality of attention and feeling that we bring to each other in affirmation of our love and gratitude. It is the creation of an environment that nurtures and supports our heart's deepest desires. Like the Sabbath, which is intended as a respite from the obligations of daily life and a means of spiritual replenishment, romance is a way of honoring the sacred space of our mutual love. Romance is a state of mind, a state of being wherein we focus our loving attention on each other in a way that interrupts the daily routines that often threaten to suffocate the flame of our love's passion.

It is easy to slip into the role of roommate, friend, business partner, and coparent. We forget to be lovers or else make it such a low priority that everything else takes precedence. We stop dating. We fail to nurture the sweet connection that once consumed us with delight and passion. We don't fall out of love; we simply allow our love to atrophy by failing to adequately attend to it. We forget that our love, like all living organisms, requires ongoing nurturance and maintenance. Keeping romance alive, in whatever forms we choose, is the antidote to the malaise that afflicts an enormous number of marriages.

As important as the romance itself is our motivation for doing it. If we act out of a sense of duty, then romance simply becomes one more obligation to fulfill. Anything done primarily out of a sense of obligation will be more likely to promote resentment and disappointment than fulfillment. The seeds of romance can be nurtured during those moments when we experience love or gratitude toward our partner. We can convert these feelings to romance by coming up with ways to honor, surprise, and delight our beloved. Romance can be a spontaneous expression of affection, or it can involve extensive plans that require great preparation.

Some people think that planning or scheduling connection

time defeats the purpose of the thrill of romance. We've found that it's possible to have regularly scheduled romance time together without losing the elements of spontaneity, surprise, and delight. In fact, the structure often enhances the experiences. Getting away and going places together can be a great way to reawaken romance, and it doesn't necessarily require a change of setting. We can rearrange our home to provide the feel of a new and different environment. Candlelight, flowers, gifts, and little surprises can contribute to creating a magical and delightful experience. One of our favorite ways to spend an evening doesn't cost anything. We take turns being in service to each other. We bathe together and wash each other's hair. We listen to our favorite music and sometimes feed each other dinner very slowly. We sit very close and make frequent physical contact with each other. We deliberately look deeply into each other's eyes and call each other pet names. After dinner, sometimes we dance together. Massage is often a part of our romance; we have a massage table and fancy scented massage oils.

The way we talk and what we talk about is extremely important. Our conversation is always sincere, intimate, and full of feeling from the heart. Talk about work, money, and responsibilities are all strictly off-limits. We focus instead primarily on what we enjoy and appreciate about each other. All these emotional interchanges are the main meal. Sex is usually the dessert, but not necessarily.

There is an infinite variety of means that you can use to bring more romance and joy into your relationship. Coming up with them together is part of the fun. If at first this practice seems awkward or uncomfortable, try to stick with it anyway. In time it will feel more natural and easy. Eventually, you won't know how you could have ever been so neglectful, and bringing more romance into your lives together will become one of the most effortless and joyful experiences of your life. Enjoy!

79

The sparkle of a
new relationship is
always temporary.

Josh and Ginger were married for eleven years with two children, aged nine and seven. Josh generally played the role of the sacrificing martyr and lived in smoldering resentment. He felt obligated to fulfill burdensome responsibilities, and he denied himself most of the experiences that had formerly brought him pleasure. He secretly blamed Ginger for his unhappiness, and she couldn't help but feel his cold, rejecting judgment of her.

Ginger was also caught up in her responsibilities as a mother, homemaker, and part-time worker outside the home. She didn't experience as strong a sense of sacrifice as Josh because she had continued to fulfill most of her personal needs throughout the marriage. A sense of deep malaise pervaded their relationship, though neither of them was willing to openly acknowledge it. It seemed easier to just continue with business as usual. One day the inevitable happened — Josh met Robyn, a young, beautiful, and single woman, unencumbered by adult responsibilities. The attraction was compelling. They began a secret relationship and continued it for nearly a year, until Josh finally told Ginger that he was leaving the marriage.

Ginger was outraged and devastated. Despite her feelings, however, she was unwilling to let go of the marriage without a fight. She tried to appeal to Josh, but his mind was made up. He wanted out. For the first time in years, he said, he felt that his life was joyful and that he was something more than just a paycheck. He couldn't risk losing this person who had brought him back from the dead. He wouldn't sacrifice his life to a stagnant, unfulfilling marriage.

When it became apparent to Ginger that Josh was closed to the idea of maintaining their marriage, she fell into deep grief. With effort and help from a good counselor, she was able to accept the loss and begin establishing a new life for herself. In ten months the divorce was final. Shortly thereafter, Josh and Robyn began experiencing difficulties that shattered their idyllic relationship. Living together proved to be very different from sustaining a secret connection. Some of the same issues and feelings of obligation that Josh experienced with Ginger began to show up in his new relationship.

In this case it was Robyn who left and refused to reconsider. To Josh's eyes, she was no longer the delightful younger woman who had freed him from his life of drudgery. In fact, she was starting to look disturbingly like Ginger. This time it was Josh who was the rejected one. It happened very quickly. According to him, "One minute we were living together, the next minute she was gone!"

In truth, none of these people had changed, but with changing circumstances, different parts of themselves began showing up. Josh experienced some painful and powerful lessons over the two-year period following his breakup from Robyn. During much of that time, he was unwilling to involve himself with any women. Gradually he was able to recover from his wounds and forgive himself for his mistakes. "Trusting myself again," he said, "is going to take some time."

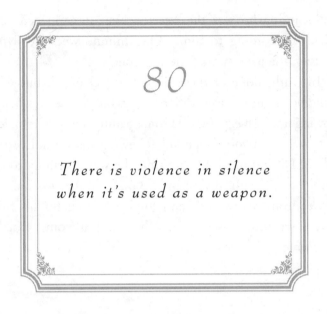

80

There is violence in silence when it's used as a weapon.

Just as our words can cut like a knife, so can silence. There are many different kinds of silence, each with a different nature, a different quality. Silence can be contemplative and thoughtful. It can be an expression of fatigue or depletion. It can be the pause between interactions when we collect our thoughts. It can be an empty space or a space of withheld anxiety or distress. What defines and determines the quality of silence is the intention that underlies it. Our silence can hold the intention to punish or to love, to reflect or to withdraw, to listen or to critique, to open or to close, to forgive or to avenge. It can be for understanding, for listening, for learning, or it can be for punishment or inflicting pain on another.

Carole was a "connection person," happiest when she

was feeling close to her husband, Al. He, however, did not always feel the same way. He didn't want to cuddle together as often as Carole did, but he found it difficult to acknowledge this and often would go along begrudgingly with her, leaving Carole frustrated and Al himself stewing in resentment and angry silence. His silence was punitive revenge for Carole "always asking so much of me." Inwardly he blamed Carole because it seemed like she was "never satisfied, no matter how much I give her."

In anger, Al closed his mouth — and his heart. His enraged silence had a violent quality that hurt Carole, just as angry words or angry actions would have. Secretly, he was pleased with her frustration and her failure to connect with him. Al ultimately paid a very high price for his unwillingness to deal more honestly with his feelings. The accumulated frustration and resentment eventually cost them the marriage.

Carole's lesson had to do with seeing that her strategy for intimacy didn't work. Rather than trying to coerce people to open up to her, she saw that she needed to give others what she wished for — responsible and respectful communication. This meant expressing her own feelings — loneliness, anxiety, frustration, sadness — and making an effort to understand the feelings of others rather than coaxing them into changing their behavior. This was no easy task, but one that she knew could in time lead to the intimacy she was seeking.

The silent treatment can be as traumatic as any aggressive, verbally abusive words. When silence is used for punishment or vindictiveness, it can trigger our partner's deepest fears of abandonment and cause them enormous suffering. On the other hand, we can use silence to pause and reflect in order to respond more skillfully. Ultimately, it is our underlying intention that determines whether our silence is beneficial or destructive.

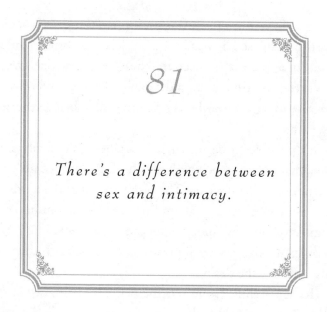

81

There's a difference between sex and intimacy.

There is desire for sex and desire for intimacy, and people often confuse the two. If one person is looking for intimacy and the other for sex, it's a setup for misunderstanding. If two partners are not aligned with the same intention, one is likely to feel dissatisfied and used.

Whenever Chad felt the desire for connection with Laura, he expressed it sexually and often ended up feeling unfulfilled. Although his physical desires would be satisfied, the pleasure tended to be short-lived. Sometimes his desire for sex would return within hours. He would then become more demanding, compulsive, and needy because his true longing was not being recognized and addressed.

When this pattern isn't interrupted, it can turn into a full-blown sex addiction. There's a saying, "You can never get enough of what you really don't want." In this case, what was missing wasn't sex, it was intimacy, deep emotional connection. But authentic connection requires genuine openness to let yourself be truly seen and known. This can be a fearful prospect to someone who is uncomfortable being emotionally vulnerable.

It's possible to be sexual without being vulnerable. Sex provides a means of being physically close, but not necessarily emotionally connected. The problem is that the more you feed someone's sexual compulsiveness by accommodating them sexually, the more addictive and demanding they become. It's like giving liquor to an alcoholic. Indulgence only inflames the desire.

To her friends, Laura was the helpless victim of her sexually insatiable husband. "He's never satisfied," she complained. "He's at me morning and night. I'm lucky if I get one day a week off." Laura tended to comply with Chad's demands, failing to set boundaries for herself. The sex inflamed Chad's desires because it wasn't satisfying. He wanted Laura to desire him, but he settled for having her body, which she grudgingly loaned him. Because he never felt wanted by her, his craving never diminished. Chad settled for empty sex when what he really wanted was deep connection. To Laura's friends she may have looked like a victim, but she was the one in the position of strength. She was the one with the power to choose whether or not to accommodate Chad's desires. It wasn't until each of them was able to identify and communicate their deeper longings and fears that Laura and Chad were able to break through this predicament.

Uncovering and expressing the deep needs that underlie sexual desire allow us to blend the experiences of sex and intimacy in a way that fulfills our hearts and souls as well as our physical bodies. Such a merging is available to all couples who are willing to make the experience of connection their highest priority.

82

It's better to focus on what you can do to make things right than on what your partner did to make things wrong.

It's always easier to see the other person's part in a problem than our own. In the middle of a breakdown, it's common to feel like a victim of what we consider to be our partner's insensitivity, selfishness, or neediness. Sometimes we feel so flooded with feelings that we can't think straight. It may take a while to calm down. As we begin to regain our rational thought processes, we can search for our own contribution and begin the process of repair.

Janet and Marty took turns being in charge of dinner. Marty loved the idea of team cooking and didn't want to be in the kitchen alone preparing the meal, but Janet saw Marty as controlling and bossy when he was the chef, and she resented his constant demands. In retaliation she would accuse him of being a poor manager, unwilling to delegate a task and let her do it her own way. Tensions would run so high that delicious meals would lose their flavor. Frustrated and resentful, Janet took to vacating the kitchen on Marty's nights to avoid the power struggles that always resulted when she tried to help.

Janet was right about the many ways Marty was contributing to the problem. When she tried to express her concerns, he became defensive and refused to listen. She was right about his being a perfectionist and that he could often be tyrannical. She was also right about his attachment to how she "should" cook the food. Her being right, however, did little to break their impasse. The more Janet focused on Marty's part in the problem, the more defensive he became. In her own way, she was being just as self-righteous, exacting, and defensive as he was.

The gridlock broke when Janet began to look at her role in the breakdown. Although she knew that Marty was being picky and unreasonable, she committed to speak only about herself, resisting the temptation to try to get him to own up to his bad behavior. She put her desire to be right aside and told Marty that she felt like a bad little girl being scolded by her dad when he expressed his judgments and disapproval so strongly. Instead of trying to get him to change, she kept expressing the feelings his behavior triggered in her.

Her sincerity and vulnerability was disarming. Marty began to open his heart, as he no longer felt defensive. Instead of anger and frustration, he started to feel empathy and compassion. His words and tone of voice softened, and he agreed to be more careful about his bossiness in the kitchen.

One courageous person can break the impasse created by blame and judgment. Being willing to be that person, rather than trying to get your partner to go first, can make the difference between prolonged suffering and openhearted connection. Sometimes you can be right *or* you can have a relationship.

83

*The fire of infatuation
has to cool before
mature love can develop.*

LINDA: Jesse, our firstborn, was three years old before I was willing to leave him for a week for a very overdue vacation alone with Charlie. To say that I had been an obsessed, over-protective, neurotic, overwhelmed mother was...well, just about right. My parents, who lived over four hundred miles away, were the only other people to whom I would entrust my baby. I wasn't totally wacko, but close.

Our destination was Martha's Vineyard. On the first night, we stayed in a bed-and-breakfast that had an antique claw-foot bathtub. I filled it with the hottest water we could stand, and we got in. We relaxed for a while, relishing the privacy, absorbed in the silence. Then Charlie washed my face with a sweet smelling soap and a soft washcloth, and I began to weep. I was the baby now, being nurtured by someone who dearly loved me. It had been a difficult transition to adulthood, with both of us working, earning degrees, and having a baby who had been more demanding than I wanted to admit. I was so tired. We knew that our honeymoon was long over, and that the intervening years had matured us and deepened our capacity for love.

Our time in the claw-foot tub may sound like an ordinary scene, but it was a pivotal communion for Charlie and me, a sharing of deep understanding, appreciation, and peace. In that bathtub, we cherished one another in a simple moment of ordinary magic. I was crying for joy for having made it to that openhearted moment. There had been so many times when I didn't know whether the marriage would survive, and if it did, whether it would embody a real appreciation for each other or an uneasy, guarded arrangement to keep the family intact. We had indeed triumphed, and now we were sitting down to rest and enjoy being free of our struggle. It was blissful!

Mature love can only come after we have been seasoned as individuals, and after the relationship has been weathered by some challenging and demanding times. No longer fettered by the unrealistic fantasies of naive new love, we bring a higher level of acceptance to our partner and ourselves. To this day, that experience in the claw-foot tub is among the most precious moments of my life.

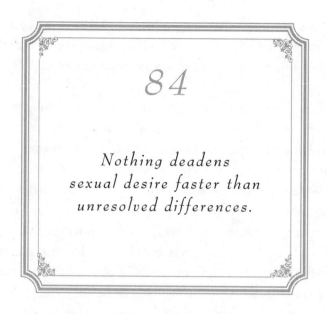

84

*Nothing deadens
sexual desire faster than
unresolved differences.*

The most significant factor in determining whether marital sex cools to a frozen impasse is not our level of technical skill and expertise, but rather our ability to keep feelings and communication open and free of unresolved differences and resentment. When negative feelings — hurt, guilt, anger, frustration — are not addressed and neutralized through honesty and understanding, they degrade the foundation of the relationship and threaten to extinguish the fire of sexual desire on one or both sides of the marriage.

Although feelings toward one's partner may cool as a result of these unaddressed issues, sexual desire is likely to continue in one or both partners and may end up directed at someone else, creating the dangerous possibility, or even likelihood, of extramarital acting out. While this might temporarily solve the "sex problem," it creates another — adultery — which is far more threatening. Allowing the relationship to deteriorate to this point puts a marriage in grave danger.

The issue is not fidelity; it's honesty. The unwillingness to tell the truth about our feelings suffocates our passion. The possibility of involvement with a prospective partner with whom we have no history is infinitely more appealing than sitting down with someone with whom we may have days, months, or even years of unresolved differences and unacknowledged feelings. Withholding these thoughts and emotions is like carrying around an enormous weight that prevents us from being elevated to the peaks of pleasure that are available when we are emotionally unencumbered.

There's a reason why great sex often follows a good fight. The expression of pent-up emotion is an aphrodisiac because it unblocks our capacity to experience feelings fully and express them directly. This is, of course, a high-risk way of connecting. "Foreplay/fightplay" is like playing with fire. Acknowledging inevitable differences as they come up will not only keep the emotional channels open, but it will also promote sexual intensity and richness. Emotional honesty will bring more passion into a relationship than roses and chocolates. Count on it.

*The biggest risk
is in not risking.*

LINDA: In the Buddhist tradition, there are four personality types — anger, greed, illusion, and fear. I've always been a fear type. Maybe I was just born that way, or maybe it's a result of childhood experiences. I don't know. Frankly, at this point I don't care. These days, the *why* questions no longer fascinate me. It's the *how* questions that are more compelling. For instance, given that I have a lot of fear to contend with, how can I best deal with it so it doesn't keep me from doing what I want to do and having the life I want to have? How can I continue to take risks, even when I'm scared? When I explore these questions, things begin to become clear for me.

I'm shy and a steady plodder. When Charlie and I were first together, my shyness prevented me from speaking up about what I really wanted out of the relationship. I shudder when I think how little I was willing to settle for in those years. My vision was seriously limited. Although in my heart I wanted the kind of open, communicative marriage that could foster a loving family, I was afraid to initiate the process of getting there. To avoid the conflict I was so afraid of, I was tempted to settle for a predictable, comfortable, and secure relationship, rather than the openhearted one I really wanted. But in the end I knew I had to risk the pain and upheaval that would come from speaking up to try and improve things. For a recovering shy person, this has been a piece of work!

During the rough patches in our marriage, there were times when I had to be willing to risk the relationship itself. I told Charlie that there were certain things that I simply couldn't live with. I didn't express this as a threat or an ultimatum, but rather as an acknowledgment of what was true for me. Sometimes I felt like I was jumping out of an airplane with no idea whether or not the parachute would open. I knew that setting my terms might drive Charlie away, but not to do so felt like a lie.

We faced the risk of losing our marriage more than once. And each time we risked it, I felt terrified. But each act of courage brought our relationship to a higher state. Today I live in gratitude for what the risks that we've taken have brought us. The results are more than I ever hoped for.

86

*If you think marriage
counseling is too expensive,
try divorce.*

This one is for people who think that it's better to wait until things get really bad before getting into marriage counseling. This is not a good idea. The time to go is sooner rather than later. The earlier one gets beneficial help, the cheaper, in terms of pain and dollars, the cost. John Gottman, the author of *How Marriages Succeed and Fail,* said in a workshop that the average couple that seeks marriage counseling experiences difficulties for six years prior to making the call! Unfortunately for all too many of them, at this point it's too late and the goodwill and caring that were present in the early stages of their relationship have eroded beyond repair. All that remains is to declare the marriage dead and give it a proper burial. When asked why they waited so long, a large percentage of these couples claimed that they felt they couldn't afford therapy and hoped that things would eventually improve on their own. This is the same kind of naive thinking that leads small children to believe that if they close their eyes, no one can see them. Not only do problems fail to disappear when we ignore them; generally they get worse. The sooner we get the help we need, the more quickly we can resolve things. In considering the difference in cost between a messy and drawn-out divorce and a typical period of marriage therapy, there's no comparison!

The sooner you get good help, the more quickly things can begin to turn around. The longer you stay entrenched in unproductive patterns, the more stuck you get and the longer it takes to become free of them. More important, the risk of reaching the point of giving up on the marriage grows with every day of unresolved pain. Doing all that you can do on your own to strengthen your marriage is always the first step, and it's often the last one. It's just as important, however, to be able to recognize when your best efforts are insufficient to heal a breakdown. It's likely that you've reached that point if repeated attempts to improve things continually result in frustration, pain, and/or resentment. If it becomes evident that your best efforts aren't working, run, don't walk, to a good marriage counselor!

There is, of course, no guarantee that getting counseling will cure what ails your marriage, but it definitely improves the odds, particularly if you can catch things in the early stages. Whatever it costs to get free from the impasses that all relationships occasionally experience, it is much cheaper in terms of money, health, and spirit to pay up front rather than after the final breakdown. Getting help when you need it might be the biggest bargain of your life!

87

*Forgiveness is
its own reward.*

LINDA: I come from a family of grudge holders. In our home it was commonplace to hear statements like "I'm not going to his daughter's college graduation! His father borrowed two thousand dollars from me in 1954 and never paid me back. I'm not having anything to do with him" or "I'm not going to Rockaway Beach for vacation" because some never-to-be-forgiven relative would be there. Someone was always not going to that wedding, that funeral, that birthday party, or on that trip, because of some slight, argument, or unpaid loan. My childhood was filled with this stuff!

Grudge holding is a learned behavior. If you observe children, you'll see lots of disputes, and the younger the kids are, the quicker they tend to get over them. Refined grudge holding takes years of training and practice. It doesn't come naturally. Hanging on to slights was a tendency that I brought into my marriage. I had no idea what it was costing me. Keeping track of the injuries consumes time and energy; it's hard to keep it all going. I didn't realize that I could choose to forgive.

Charlie, on the other hand, is different. It wasn't that I never let him down or made any mistakes; I made plenty. But his style is to express himself in a burst of feeling and then it's over, whereas I tend toward the long-suffering mode. At a certain point, our relationship was in danger of toppling because I was so heavily laden with bitterness, resentment, and unfulfilled expectations. Charlie was not about to change his stance. It was up to me to find a way out of the dilemma.

I learned forgiveness meditation from Stephen and Ondrea Levine, two wonderfully gifted spiritual teachers, and I began the practice of letting go. I had to work at it, as forgiveness can only be accomplished in stages, not all in a single sitting. Since nothing inspires one to succeed like success, as soon as I experienced the rewards of forgiveness — a feeling of lightness and freedom — it pushed me on to do more. As my heart was opening, I was able to enjoy the brief time I did have with Charlie rather than wasting it by marinating in resentment about how little we saw each other. Forgiving is the most powerful tool I have ever found for cleansing a toxic relationship of the poison of resentment. For many of us, it is one of the most important skills we will ever develop.

88

*Revenge is its
own punishment.*

CHARLIE: There are few criticisms that provoke more defensiveness than the accusation of being "vengeful." For most of us, this is a particularly nasty attribute, even more negative than being egotistical, selfish, lazy, or controlling. To be vengeful is to deliberately seek to cause harm or suffering to someone who we think has wronged us. It's not easy to acknowledge, but we are being vengeful whenever we strike out in reaction to our experience of being injured. Every time we use our words to punish, control, or retaliate against someone, we are being vengeful. I used to think that because I never lifted a finger to physically harm Linda, I was not a vengeful person. I took solace in this and even felt a kind of smugness and superiority, until I realized that the violence of my words was no less destructive than the actions I prided myself in not taking. I came to understand that my desire to "get Linda to understand" or to "make my point" or to convince her that I was right were often no more than ill-concealed efforts to punish her.

This realization was humbling and shameful to me, and it forced me to not only confront this shadow part of myself, but to see the price that I was paying for being vengeful, for lashing out, whenever I felt attacked, scared, or wounded. Acting or speaking from that impulse inevitably left me feeling shut down, mistrusting, closed-hearted, and isolated. It wasn't Linda's behavior that caused me to feel these things; it was my own defensiveness and reactivity. The more I indulged myself, the more justified I felt in being vengeful.

When I realized that I was the cause of my pain, that I was responsible, my vengeful instincts lost their power. Although the tendency to lash out verbally still arises from time to time, I am no longer consumed by it — not because I think it is the wrong thing to do, but because I am no longer willing to cause myself this kind of pain. It wasn't until I truly saw that it was I, not Linda, who was creating my own personal prison that I could take back the power to free myself and move from hell to happiness.

89

When two hearts are connected, the biggest problems become workable; when they are not, the smallest difficulties seem insurmountable.

LINDA: We often don't realize how precariously we are perched in our life. In an instant, our whole existence can change. We may be going along innocently when we get into a car accident or get a phone call telling us that someone dear to us has died. We may suddenly become ill or discover some truth that had been kept secret from us, and from that moment on nothing is the same.

This is what happened to me in 1991 when I was diagnosed with metastatic breast cancer. Within a few days of my diagnosis, I was in the hospital for the lumpectomy. After that, I went right into the chemotherapy regimen, followed by radiation. I lost all my hair from chemotherapy, and I experienced severe mood swings as a side effect of the hormonal disruption following chemotherapy. My entire life as

I had known it was turned upside-down. As a "bonus," I got to look death straight in the eyes for the first time in my life. There was no doubt that this was one hell of a challenge.

But it wasn't the biggest one I had ever confronted. Believe it or not, the cancer challenge was a lot easier than others I had faced because I didn't feel alone with it. The cancer diagnosis came at a time when Charlie and I were especially close; I call it our "Golden Age." We had previously experienced times of deep darkness in our relationship and come close to divorce. Looking back on the things that we used to fight over, it's hard to imagine that such trivia could have been so upsetting. Arguing over who would do the dishes, call the babysitter, choose which video to rent, do the laundry, clean up the cat vomit, or who should apologize first now seems absurdly petty and insignificant. I know now that the protracted power struggle that surrounded these issues persisted because we were not joined heart to heart.

During my bout with cancer, both Charlie and I were able to be more open and accepting of each other and ourselves. That made quite a difference. I was weakened by the chemotherapy, and also by the intensity of my fear of death. Charlie was terrified that he could lose me so early in life. We were not ready to lose each other, especially after working so hard to come so far. During the several months surrounding my treatments, Charlie stayed close to my side. He showed me in every possible way that he loved me: he would touch me frequently, take my hand, hold me in his arms, listen for hours to what I was thinking and feeling, and speak to me from the depths of his heart.

Only the most significant of issues registered on our radar screen. Trivial issues had no weight. In the face of death, only matters of love and caring held any importance for us. I feel quite certain that if my diagnosis had come during one of the periods where our marriage was unstable, the shock of cancer would have destroyed our marriage. I would have decided to leave to save my own life. Thank goodness the illness instead came when we were strong enough together to meet the challenge. We have had other crises and difficulties in the last several years, and we handle them by focusing on what's most important in life, with the grace that comes from being profoundly connected to ourselves and each other.

90

Constructive criticism
generally isn't.

CHARLIE: "Can I give you some feedback?" If your partner proposes this to you, beware. Most of the time this seemingly harmless offer conceals a not-so-hidden intention that is anything but supportive. What often underlies the offer for feedback is a desire to advise, criticize, judge, or control another person by giving an opinion that elevates the speaker to the superior position. What I used to refer to as "feedback" was usually nothing more than criticism and advice that often would leave Linda feeling put down and inferior. Although I would insist that I was only "telling you this to help you," my words rarely had that effect. More often than not, Linda would cringe whenever I offered this so-called help. She eventually told me to keep it to myself unless she asked for it.

Sometimes I would tell Linda that she shouldn't feel put down, which was as unproductive as the criticism itself, and we would proceed to engage in a dialogue that usually ended with both of us feeling frustrated and misunderstood. The problem usually had more to do with what was motivating my words than the words themselves. By criticizing Linda under the guise of feedback, I was negating her feelings and thoughts. I always viewed myself as right, and I thought that if Linda had any sense at all, she would listen to me and take my words seriously. No wonder she hated accepting my input. It was filled with embedded judgments, blame, and unsolicited advice. She was right to trust herself and recoil from my feedback. In her gut, she knew that despite my words, my intention wasn't trustworthy.

These days I tend to distrust my intentions whenever I feel a strong desire to criticize or advise Linda or anyone else. Rather than acting on my initial impulse, I'm more likely to pause for a moment to ask myself what I'm trying to accomplish and who I'm really looking out for. Is it the other person or my ego in disguise? If, upon reflection, it looks like I'm primarily concerned with serving the other person, and I have reason to believe that they desire my input, I'll offer it as nonjudgmentally as I can. If I don't trust my motivation, I'll keep my mouth shut. Sometimes the most helpful and loving thing we can do is resist the temptation to offer feedback, recognizing that such criticism wouldn't be constructive at all, and instead offer our caring and loving attention.

91

The capacity to feel joy grows in proportion to the capacity to experience pain.

Our friend Jody is dedicated to going after whatever she thinks will bring her more pleasure and joy, and, just as deliberately, avoiding anything that might cause her distress or unhappiness. Her favorite phrases are "Go for the joy," "Choose happiness," and "Fear is just a four-letter word." If anyone I know is "following her bliss," it's Jody.

Jody's life, however, is anything but blissful. In her pursuit of happiness, she religiously avoids "anything or anyone that makes me feel bad, sad, or mad." She leaves relationships with romantic partners and friends as soon as they become difficult (and at some point they always do). She relentlessly tries to cheer people up because she has so little tolerance for their struggles and suffering. She leaves jobs when they become stressful, rather than learning to deal with the stress. The problem with Jody's life strategy is that because she has little experience coming to grips with the shadow side of life, her capacity to experience real joy is deeply diminished.

Life and relationships are a package deal, which include rain *and* shine. To the degree that we try to avoid or exclude that which brings us unhappiness, our capacity for joy is correspondingly limited. It is the intense feelings — good and bad — that stretch our hearts ever more open and deepen our capacity to live fully and experience joy, as well as connection to our partner. Like muscle fibers that are broken down through an intense physical workout and then knitted back together to be stronger and more resilient than before, the heart's capacity to hold deep and powerful feelings expands when we embrace, rather than resist, the full measure of our emotions. Thus we become increasingly able to manage and hold the most intense feelings, both good and bad. The strength and support of loving friends and helpers who can meet us where we are further deepens us. This quality of the heart's resilience prompts and allows us to keep ourselves open, even during the most trying of times.

Jody's unwillingness to deeply experience her feelings reflects her fear of being consumed by them. Trying to avoid the painful feelings has left her unequipped to handle them. When we are willing to risk encountering ourselves openly and fearlessly, we build the courage and confidence necessary to welcome the full range and depth of our emotional experience. In so doing, our heart is stretched open to hold greater joy than we otherwise could have known.

92

*There is no greater
eloquence than the silence
of real listening.*

CHARLIE: Like many males, I grew up believing that it was my job to keep my woman happy. This meant figuring out what was bothering her when she seemed upset and doing something to remedy the situation — give advice, change the light bulb, explain things, yell at the store clerk who had been rude to her, fix the flat, whatever it would take to make her feel better. I grew up, got married, and applied this strategy in my marriage. Sometimes it worked and Linda would end up feeling better, but often it didn't. When Linda didn't appreciate my efforts or advice, I would often feel resentful and unappreciated. After all, wasn't I giving her what she wanted and needed? Why else would she bother telling me that she was upset about something unless she wanted me to do something about it?

One day, in a fit of frustration, I actually asked Linda that question. We had just left a social event in which she had felt snubbed by one of the guests. As Linda was expressing her feelings, I was already rehearsing my response. I was driving, listening to the radio, listening to Linda, and listening to my mental strategy to *fix* her so that she would feel better and I would once again feel like a competent and helpful husband.

Before Linda could finish telling me what she was feeling, I jumped right in with my insight and advice. It was designed, of course, to get her to see that she shouldn't take things so personally. The guy at the party was obviously a jerk and his opinion shouldn't mean anything to her, I reasoned, so why doesn't she just listen to me and get over it? This may not be a verbatim account of what I said, but it's pretty close. Linda's response was, "That's not what I need to hear. That doesn't make me feel better." That was not what *I* wanted to hear. "If you don't want me to try to help you to feel better," I responded, "why are you telling me this in the first place?"

It wasn't actually spoken as a question, and it wasn't said in a very caring way. The underlying message was more like "What the hell is the matter with you? Here I am trying to respond to your request for help and all you can do is tell me that my input isn't good enough! What do you want from me, anyway?" I was so obviously angry that Linda refused to continue the discussion while we were driving and insisted that we wait until we get home to resume it. This made me even more upset, but since Linda wouldn't engage me I just fumed for the rest of the drive.

I was still upset when we got home, but in the silence of the previous twenty minutes I had become aware of my true feelings — the hurt and rejection beneath my resentment. I had cooled down enough to listen to Linda without being so defensive. We went upstairs to the bedroom and sat down together. She was the first to speak.

"I'm sorry that you feel so upset by what I said, but it is important to me that you understand what I am really needing now. I don't want you to tell me something that will change my feelings. I just want to feel that you are with me, that you understand what I'm experiencing so that I don't feel so alone with my emotions. I want to feel you *with* me. I want your whole attention. In the car there was so much going on I felt like I was only getting a sliver of your attention, but what I wanted was *all* of it, all of *you*. I probably should have waited until we got home to even bring this up, but I was anxious to tell you, not so that you could fix it, but so that I could feel heard and understood by you, and feel connected to you. That's what I need. That's what really helps."

"So you never want me to help you to feel better or see things differently if I think that that might be helpful to you?" I asked. I was still hurting and defensive.

"That's not what I'm saying. Sometimes I do want you to give me your input, and often when you do that's very helpful. But this time I just wanted your full attention, because that's what really comforts me. When you're busy trying to come up with the 'right' response I don't feel connected with you. When I want you to give me advice or perspective, I'll let you know. If I don't ask for it, then assume that I don't want it. I just want you to let me know that you're with me."

Finally, I was beginning to hear what Linda was saying. There was stillness between us that felt full and loving. Linda reached out to take my hand. I felt grateful for the moment and relieved in my awareness that I didn't have to solve her problems or end her pain, but simply be open to her and allow myself to be moved by her feelings. I reached out and held her in gratitude and love. This was not the last time that I needed to be reminded by Linda that I didn't need to fix her. After all, patterns of a lifetime don't disappear overnight. It was, however, the last time that I got angry with her for reminding me that I didn't need to "do" anything, except put everything aside and be there with her. Today her reminders leave me feeling relieved rather than criticized, and we both agree that I am becoming a world-class listener.

93

*External conflicts are often
outer expressions of
internal ones.*

LINDA: Like many of the couples with whom we've worked, an area of great conflict for Charlie and me over the years was child raising. Our orientations toward discipline, for example, have always been quite different. Charlie has always had a hands-off approach and has tended toward the laissez-faire end of the parenting spectrum. He calls his attitude "relaxed." I used to call it "overly permissive." I, on the other hand, have always been more strict and structured in my approach. I see myself as "responsible." He calls it "controlling."

In time, we recognized how our differing perspectives helped us to provide a more balanced family environment than we would have had otherwise, and we eventually came to appreciate our differences rather than trying to eliminate them. A direct consequence of these differences was that it was hard to get the kids to help out around the house. Charlie wouldn't oppose my efforts to enlist their help, but he wouldn't take the kind of a stand that I thought was needed. Consequently, not only did the kids get off the hook a lot (in my opinion), but I was continually feeling overworked and resentful. One of my recurrent complaints was, "I need some more help around here. I'm working and doing most of the cooking, and the dishes, too." Charlie would say he agreed, but he didn't do much about it. I felt like a beast of burden, laden down with saddlebags.

At some point, something inside me just clicked. I had been arguing with Charlie, trying to get him to get Jesse to do his dishes, when I realized what the problem was. The real fight was within myself. Some part of me was still hanging on to trying to be a "milk and cookies" mom who cooks and does dishes, a homemaker like my own mother, even though, unlike her, I had a full-time career. Two aspects of my personality were at war inside me. So I called a family meeting. I taped a chart to the refrigerator door with nightly cooking and dishwashing assignments for every family member. "I won't be cooking except on my designated nights, and I won't be doing dishes except on my designated nights." My voice had the ring of resolve, and everyone got it.

Of course I was tested, and some nights we all sat at the table with nothing to eat while someone scrambled to create a meal at the last minute. But after a transition, the cooking and dish night schedule fell into place. It was a happy day when Charlie said playfully, "Don't touch that pan, those are Sarah's dishes."

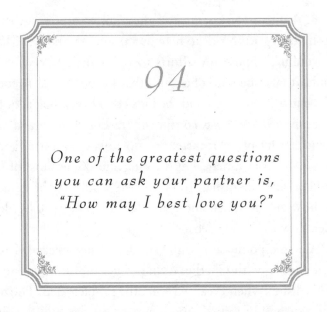

94

*One of the greatest questions
you can ask your partner is,
"How may I best love you?"*

One afternoon's back-to-back appointments demonstrated that different individuals can need strikingly different things in order to feel loved. In the first session, Claire sobbed that she didn't feel loved by her husband, Matt. He, in turn, expressed bewilderment and frustration, stating that he just couldn't understand why she was carrying on this way. After being questioned further, Claire, still sniffling, said, "You never tell me that you love me." Matt had been under the impression that making a good living and supporting the family, along with all of the other actions that he took, were sufficient to demonstrate his love for his wife. He knew how much he loved her and assumed she knew it too. He was introverted and shy and unaccustomed to speaking openly about his feelings. During the session, with awkwardness and effort, he finally did manage to say "I love you." The words were music to Claire's ears. She hadn't heard them for years.

The next couple came in grappling with the same issue. Jeanette stated that she did not feel loved by her husband, Patrick. She said, "You are always telling me that you love me, but I wish you'd show it with your actions. I hate having to pick up after you all the time. I wish you would pick up your socks, put your dirty dishes in the sink, and stop leaving your wet towels on the bed. You say you love me, but you don't seem to hear a thing I say!" Words were definitely not what she was looking for. She wanted action.

We all have specific ways that we want to experience being loved. We tend to give what we want to receive; we can't help being subjective. Wise lovers remember to ask each other, pay close attention, and generally act on the input they receive.

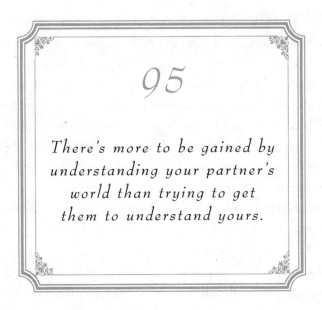

95

There's more to be gained by understanding your partner's world than trying to get them to understand yours.

LINDA: One time in the midst of one of our early arguments, out of the blue Charlie looked deeply into my eyes and asked, "What do you need from me right now? I really want to know." His sudden and profound presence caught me off-guard, and it definitely got my attention. There was no anger or judgment in his voice, just a sincere desire to know me better in this moment. I felt disarmed and emotional, as though I could cry. "Just touch me. Please hold me in your arms," I said. Wordlessly, he responded and gently wrapped his arms around me. As he did, whatever had been bothering me melted away. It was like healing salve on a wound; in an instant, everything was better. It wasn't the words, it was the way he said them, his response. He extended his caring to me in recognition of my discomfort.

He stretched into my world, with sincerity and curiosity; he wanted to know me, not just shut me up. I felt it, and it was like water to someone dying of thirst.

We had already traveled most of the distance to where I wanted our relationship to be, connected heart to heart. I felt accepted with my needs, and I was grateful that the most important person in my life cared enough, was big enough, strong enough, loving enough, to want to know my needs and respond to them. I was no longer alone.

96

A loving marriage can heal old emotional wounds more effectively than the best therapy.

CHARLIE: At its best, psychotherapy creates a warm and understanding relationship through which we face ourselves and our feelings honestly in a way that allows us to heal from past wounds and accept ourselves as we are. It is the therapist's very being, rather than their philosophy or orientation, that promotes this process. The best therapists are not distinguished by their degrees or credentials, but by their ability to extend themselves nonjudgmentally with openness, authenticity, and compassion. One doesn't learn these qualities in graduate school but instead cultivates them through deliberate choice and life experience.

Although marriage doesn't require you to take on the role of therapist, it does require both partners to develop the personal qualities of a good therapist. While few of us come into a relationship with these attributes fully developed, the cauldron of marriage provides us the context through which we can explore and enrich these aspects of ourselves.

Linda's commitment to becoming a more loving person has helped me to accept myself in ways that I could never have accomplished on my own. Her willingness to view me (not always, but frequently) through eyes of compassion and acceptance eventually overrode my deeply embedded negative self-judgments. Over time, I came to see myself through her eyes and was able to find forgiveness for my perceived deficiencies, and acceptance of my "imperfections." This allowed me to experience genuine self-love for the first time in my adult life.

Linda's capacity to lovingly extend herself grew over time and with practice. And as it did, I became increasingly more able to return her gift with gratitude and help her to transform her own self-perception in a similar way. While marriage cannot be a substitute for counseling or therapy, we are both living proof that it can promote the maturation process in profound and powerful ways.

97

Just keep talkin'.

LINDA: Once when I was on a plane flying to Little Rock, Arkansas, I found myself seated next to an older woman. I remember her as having kind, intelligent eyes. We struck up a conversation, and she seemed delighted to find out I was on my way to facilitate a workshop for couples. She was on her way to teach a seminar on forgiveness. Seeing that we had much in common, we quickly fell into an animated conversation. When I mentioned that I often taught with my husband, her mood changed and she became melancholy. She told me that her husband had died four years earlier and that she still missed him terribly. They had been married for forty-six years. She had tears in her eyes as she spoke, and I was deeply touched by how open she was about the beauty of their life together.

At one point, I gently asked, "What was the secret of your long, happy marriage?" "Just keep talkin'," she said with barely a moment's hesitation. "I beg your pardon?" I said, waiting for more of an explanation. She repeated herself, "Just keep talkin'. No matter how late it is, no matter how frustrated you are, no matter how tired you are, no matter what you'd rather do, if you're not feeling good toward each other, just keep talkin' until you do." We both laughed and I promised that I would tell my class. I quoted her that weekend, and many times since.

So often couples give up in resignation when they don't feel understood. There is so much miscommunication and distortion, taboos, sensitivity, and missed opportunities. Sometimes, we have to go over the same topic a hundred times, in different ways, from different vantage points, before we can reach real understanding. Each conversation can be like filing down rough edges where we get snagged. The secret seems to be in not quitting. "Just keep talkin'!" is a simple and profound wisdom.

98

*Assumptions are fine,
as long as you check them out
before acting on them.*

Sandy and Bay had been together for three years, and they were blissfully happy during most of that time. This was a couple with a great deal of compatibility. They had easygoing temperaments and similar interests, they were considerate, warm, and affectionate, and the sex was great. They spoke openly and happily about the prospect of marriage.

There was, however, one problem — they had never talked about having children. Sandy just assumed that since everything else in their relationship was so smooth that when the time came for marriage and children, that would just flow too. When Bay said, "I'm not planning to ever have any children," Sandy was shocked and speechless. She had never asked, she had assumed. She told Bay that it was unthinkable for her to forgo children and that she was going to have to leave the relationship; he didn't protest. It was a bitter lesson.

Most assumptions are not so dramatic as Sandy's, but a series of small, misguided assumptions can also cause struggle and frustration. Asking clarifying questions of your partner and being clear and forthcoming yourself allows for a more comprehensive understanding.

99

Marriages can stay fresh
over time.

Madelyn and Steve were participants in a workshop we taught several years ago. Madelyn dressed conservatively and wore no makeup. She was a librarian and Steve was an accountant, and they had been married for twenty-two years. Although on the surface there was nothing particularly striking about this couple, they had a special vitality between them that you couldn't help but notice. I was so delighted by a story they told me during a break in the workshop that I had them tell it again to the whole class.

While Steve was out of town for two weeks on business, Madelyn took the time to reflect a bit about how marriages can slide into complacency and predictability. She knew it was time to do something out of the ordinary to refresh their relationship. She went to a friend's house to borrow clothes that were entirely out of character for her. Although she had long shapely legs, she didn't own even one miniskirt. Her friend loaned her a very short skirt, a heavily padded push-up bra, a skimpy, low-cut tank top, fishnet stockings, and stiletto heels. She rented a long, platinum blond wig and got a manicure with long acrylic nails covered with purple polish.

On the day of Steve's return, he was planning to take the airport shuttle home, as he usually did. But Madelyn showed up at the airport in her risqué attire, wig, heavy makeup, and purple nails. When Steve got off the plane, she walked up to him and in a convincing Australian accent said, "Want a date, mate?"

Steve swore to us that he didn't know it was Madelyn. He said he felt that there was something vaguely familiar about the woman, as if he may have seen her somewhere before. He just shook his head and kept walking toward the baggage claim. She persisted and kept talking to him in the Aussie accent. Finally Steve caught on. They happily reported that they did not go home after leaving the airport. Instead, they went to a motel and had an entirely lascivious time. We got the message.

There is much to learn from Madelyn and Steve's story. We need to pay attention to our relationship and not allow routine and predictability to dominate it. To keep a relationship fresh, we need to step out of character from time to time and give and receive the gift of novelty and innovation.

100

*Intention may not be
the only thing, but it's the
most important thing.*

LINDA: There have been many times when I have felt over-whelmed and confused, not knowing how to heal a rift between Charlie and me. I've been flooded with anger, sad-ness, or some other powerful emotion. Possessed by these feelings, I couldn't think straight. I felt like a little boat bob-bing up and down in a raging storm, desperately trying to get safely home again. "Home" might mean reconnecting with Charlie, or feeling secure and peaceful within myself, or just free from pain or confusion. At times, all I had was my intention. My commitment was to have a healthy relation-ship, to be close to Charlie and still hang onto myself. Early in our marriage, I certainly did not know much about how to do that. But I had my intention and I clung to it.

I remember arguing over one of our many irreconcilable

differences. I wanted the two of us to go away alone for the weekend; Charlie wanted the kids to come along. My greater commitment was to having respect and cooperation in our marriage, so I held fast to my intention as to the mast of a ship so the storm wouldn't sweep me overboard into the dark night sea. I was able to stay steady and open to Charlie's input without getting seduced by the desire to win the argument. We stayed with it until we agreed to take two weekends away, one with the children, and one without. And things didn't deteriorate into a struggle over which trip we would take first. We didn't get thrown overboard.

In a particularly violent storm, we may even have to lash ourselves to the mast. One can easily see how the challenges of relationship can threaten to throw us into the sea. If we don't have good communication skills to express the truth of our experience, we can fall in. If we can't negotiate with our partner and respond to their needs, we can fall in. If we don't learn to be strong and courageous enough to keep our balance when the unpredictable erupts, we can fall in. If we're tight, rigid, unforgiving, and inflexible, over we go. There are skills we must learn, and once we learn them it is likely to be an exhilarating ride.

The path through the storms has taken a thousand different turns. It has been my powerful commitment to intimacy with Charlie and my depth of purpose in holding on to myself that have seen me through. Intention is an awesome power, greater than most of us realize. It has gotten us through rough seas that otherwise would have sunk or grounded us for sure.

101

*The amount of joy and
fulfillment available in
a loving partnership
is considerably more
than you can imagine.*

CHARLIE: Abraham Maslow was a developmental psychologist who stressed that it was important to study not only those people who suffer from mental health problems, but also those who best exemplify the greatness that humans can achieve. He used the term "self-actualization" to refer to the highest level of functioning that a person can attain. He claimed that given the right conditions and sufficient motivation, a person can fulfill their highest potential.

To develop our latent capacities, we need "believing eyes." We need the people around us who can see the beauty, talent, and possibility that we cannot recognize in ourselves, people who nurture our best qualities and are willing to confront us about our less developed areas. We need fertile ground to fully flourish. My friend Seymour speaks about each of us being a perfect diamond, covered with dirt; it is the friction — the agitation, aggravation, and conflict — of relationships that rubs the encrusted crud off the surface of the diamond.

In this transformative process, we don't change into someone other than who we are; rather, we more fully embody our basic nature. Our partner can not only accompany us in this process, but they can assist us to move into states of being that we have not previously known. My life has taken on a quality of ease, trust, playfulness, and joy that was inconceivable to me only ten years ago. It is far beyond anything I thought I had a right to expect. The biggest challenge these days is in allowing these experiences to grow even deeper and to share them with increasing numbers of people. Now I can see that this is a possibility for anyone who chooses to embark on this incredible journey of awakening. It is available to everyone — not just those who come from happy families or are brilliant or gifted — as long as they possess an intention to learn about themselves and their relationships with others.

My most frequent answer to the question, "Why did you put up with so much pain and difficulty in the early stages of your marriage?" is "Because I knew it would be worth it!" I am convinced that there would be a lot fewer divorces if couples could somehow get a glimpse of the rewards available to those who hang in there and do the work necessary to cocreate an authentically loving marriage. The problem with many of us is not that we desire too much from marriage, but rather expect too little. More often than not, we greatly underestimate the possibilities for love, joy, freedom, and wholeness that two partners in this creative process can generate for themselves, each other, and the world around them. The real question is not "How much pain are you willing to tolerate?" but "How much joy are you willing to experience?"

About the Authors

Linda Bloom, L.C.S.W., and Charlie Bloom, M.S.W., have been assisting individuals, couples, and organizations in the process of developing wholeness and integrity since 1975. They are the founders and codirectors of Bloomwork, and they have lectured and taught seminars on relationships since 1986 to thousands of people throughout the United States and in overseas locations including China, Brazil, India, Japan, Indonesia, and Bangladesh. They are regular presenters at the Esalen Institute in Big Sur, California, and they have been adjunct faculty members at the California Institute of Integral Studies, the Omega Institute, JFK University, the Institute of Transpersonal Psychology, the

University of California at Berkeley Extension Program, Antioch University, and many other institutes of higher learning.

Charlie and Linda have been married since 1972 and have raised three children. They live in northern California.

Contact Us

Some of the stories that you read in this book were submitted by friends. We would love to hear your story, so we invite you to contribute some insight that you have realized through your marriage. We might use it in a future book or article, and we will be sure that you are credited for the submission.

To submit a story, or for information regarding Bloomwork, including training activities, tapes, publications, and scheduling, or to be placed on the Bloomwork mailing list, please contact:

Bloomwork
P.O. Box 2187
Sonoma, CA 95476
707-939-1139 • website: www.bloomwork.com